BIRTH OF A
NEW CONSC

Dialogues with the Sidhe

Jaap van Etten, PhD

Other books by Jaap Van Etten

Crystal Skulls:
Interacting with a Phenomenon

Crystal Skulls:
Expand Your Consciousness

Gifts of Mother Earth:
Earth Energies, Vortexes, Lines, and Grids

BIRTH
OF A
NEW
CONSCIOUSNESS

Dialogues with the Sidhe

Jaap van Etten, PhD

For more information about special discounts for bulk purchases, please contact
Light Technology Publishing Special Sales at 1-800-450-0985, 1-928-526-1345, or
publishing@LightTechnology.net.

Cover art: *Encounter in Wistman's Wood* by Cheryl Yambrach Rose

✳   ✳   ✳

ISBN-13: 978-1-62233-033-1

Light Technology Publishing, LLC
Phone: 800-450-0985 • 928-526-1345
Fax: 928-714-1132
PO Box 3540
Flagstaff, AZ 86003
www.lighttechnology.com

I dedicate this book to Gaia, who never gives up on the human species, not even after all the damage humans have done to her system.

CONTENTS

✑ Chapter 11 ✑

✑ Chapter 12 ✑

✑ Chapter 13 ✑

ACKNOWLEDGMENTS

The two Sidhe (pronounced *shee*) I collaborated with to write this book have become close and dear friends. Knowing now that Sidhe generally do not like to connect closely with humans, I feel especially honored and grateful that they were willing to do so with me and to start the project that resulted in this book. Thank you, ShaRaEl and KiRaEl, for your trust and openness. Our explorations have been very exciting and have changed my life. I will be forever grateful.

I would like to thank Daniel Maddux for guiding me into the area where I had my first contact with the Sidhe. Thanks to you, I dared to go where I would never have gone without you. Our hikes into the canyons have been essential for making deeper connections with the Sidhe. Without these hikes, this book would never have been written. You have been a wonderful support and a great hiking buddy.

I would like to thank Deborah Downs and my beloved Jeanne Michaels whose enthusiasm for the subtle worlds led to the creation of a small group that decided to explore aspects of those worlds. Through the stimulation of this group, I connected more deeply with the Sidhe, which led to the unfoldment of this connection and the writing of this book. The other members of the group, who I'd also like to thank, are Sandi O'Connor, Diana Rodriguez, Ssuzanne

Grandon, Rhonda Pallas Downey, Kat Breazeale, Jeannette Ramos, and Sarah and Sophia Hermosillo.

I would like to thank those who helped me to transform my sometimes funny Dutch-English into an acceptable form for my publisher. First, I would like to thank my wonderful wife, Jeanne Michaels, for her willingness to edit the worst deformations from the manuscript. I would also like to thank Sandi O'Connor and Deborah Downs for their willingness to read the manuscript and add their comments, which helped to improve it even more. Thank you, Kristina Arysta, for being a great editor, for always being supportive of my projects, and for the wonderful exchanges we've shared.

I would like to thank Light Technology Publishing. Thank you, Melody, for your willingness to publish yet another one of my books, and thank you, Light Technology Publishing team, for your efforts in creating another book of which I am proud to share with the world.

Although I have thanked her a couple of times, I would like to express my gratitude one more time to Jeanne Michaels, my wonderful wife. You had to deal with me when I went through some challenging times. I always felt your love, your support, and your belief in me. It means more to me than I can describe.

Finally, I would like to thank Gaia. Throughout the project I have felt your presence and your support. Thank you for your trust in me.

INTRODUCTION

To begin, I have a rather unusual request: Please do not skip this introduction. Given the nature of this book — dialogues with invisible beings who live in the same system as we do but who are unfamiliar to most people — I have used this section, especially the second half, to give information that will help you to understand the content of this book. Consequently, reading this introduction will make reading this book more beneficial.

I am surprised that I am willing and able to write a book like the one you hold in your hands. John Matthews's book about the Sidhe[1] started similarly to this. The Sidhe seem to affect people in this way. One moment I had my first contact, and the next, I was sitting behind the computer, typing as fast as I could with two fingers (yes, I still type with only two fingers) to input the information they asked me to share as clearly and quickly as possible. It was not always a comfortable process, but it definitely was an interesting one.

I find that I often surrender to whatever is happening, which gives the impression that there is no alternative. However, I realize that I chose to embark on this journey with the Sidhe, no matter how strange and seemingly beyond my volition. The energy to connect was so strong that I chose to surrender to the flow. It was a strange feeling to find myself suddenly communicating with beings I had just met and hardly knew, yet quickly there was a familiarity that surprised me. There was an increasing curiosity to know where our sharing and dialogues would lead. I am not disappointed and am willing to reconnect should the opportunity present itself.

Looking back, I am aware that the Sidhe and I were only players in a larger process. The second time I met the two Sidhe who were my contacts with their world, I also met another consciousness that was very powerful: Gaia. At that time, I did not understand what she was trying to tell me. I now know that she came to encourage the connection between the Sidhe and me. As you read this book, you will understand that the results of what was shared are very important for Gaia and for all life that exists within her system. She stimulated the title *Birth of a New Consciousness*. She was crystal clear about this new consciousness. For Gaia's system to unfold as it is meant to, the Sidhe and humans must cocreate a new consciousness that will make the necessary shift possible. We, the Sidhe and humans, have a responsibility to raise the vibration of Gaia to allow her purpose and all that exists within her to unfold.

I am grateful for Gaia's support. In the beginning, I resisted because I feared that this would be a duplicate of what had been written by others such as John Matthews[1] and David Spangler.[2] However, both Gaia and the Sidhe convinced me that each book has its own role to fulfill. The interaction between the Sidhe and humans is so preliminary that they need different people with different perspectives to ensure that the information they want to share will become available. The Sidhe also felt that they needed to change the form of communication to be shared. They wanted me to share my ideas so that our communication was more of a dialogue. They believed that this type of interaction would bring our two races closer together. Looking at the results, I am glad I did not follow my impulse to back out and that I listened to Gaia when she asked me to continue.

The first phase of staying in contact with the Sidhe while I typed the information was very intense for me. It was as if I were temporarily taken over. It became compulsion to get the information written down as quickly as possible. This made it difficult to do anything other than type. These obsessive tendencies felt unpleasant at times. Once everything was written down, I understood why it had to happen that way. The obsession that kept me in a permanent state of connection was required to finish this project. Thanks to this need, it was possible to write a text that came from a deep level of connection. I am able to reinstate the connection with the two Sidhe, but it is not easy, and it is less intense than during the period of typing.

As you will see, this book is not just about the Sidhe. It is equally about humans, and it offers a look at our world from a different perspective. In fact, it is always about us. We need to determine whether specific information helps us on our journey. We have a responsibility to become who we truly are. Currently, we are a people locked in a world that tells us who we ought to be. This disempowering situation has completely messed up the world we live in. Although we are aware of this to various degrees, we seem to be unable to do much about it as a species. Collectively, we feel powerless. In order to change, we need to see the world and ourselves from a different perspective. The Sidhe's perspective can help us decide to change.

As you read my responses to the Sidhe when they asked me to share my way of looking at the subjects they wanted to talk about, it might seem that what I shared was harsh and judgmental. It is, however, not my intent to judge. My intent is to offer a reflection of what I perceive we have created in our world. It can be summarized succinctly as a mess. We are a species that is capable of killing members of our own kind without any reason other than seeing them as different. I see a polluted world with no clear signs that this will change soon. I see a species that has the capability to blow up this planet that is its home, unwilling to let go of that capability. Yes, I might sound harsh. However, I am kind compared to others.

When I was writing this part of the introduction, I received an article from Richard Cassaro[3] in which he describes America as an Orwellian nightmare. Cassaro is only one of many examples. It is important to state that I, in addition to Cassaro, am talking about the collective consciousness. I am aware that there are individuals and small groups who are changing to some degree and no longer completely fit the patterns of the collective.

This book, as is the case with all of my books, does not claim to present *the* truth. I do not know what the ultimate truth is because truth is held by Source. As human beings living in this reality, we can connect with aspects of truth, and by sharing with each other, we build a larger perspective of it. I share what I believe and what feels right for me to share in the moment that I write it. I leave it to the readers to decide which aspects of the information resonate. Never give away your power to anyone — not any writing, any sharing, or any being. The tendency to give away our power has created the world we live in today. We want less disempowerment, not more! This book invites you to feel your own truth and to empower yourself.

SIDHE REPETITION

Are you willing to go deeper? There seems to be much repetition in the book. The Sidhe repeat certain subjects many times. However, they do this for a reason. In the first place, repetition is used as part of something new. Second, the repetition is meant to create an energy field that brings us increasingly closer together. Personally, I was afraid that the repetition might irritate people. The Sidhe, however, found it important, and I decided to leave it to the readers to feel what effect it has on them. However, I was still not completely at ease with it. When I brought up the subject again, they shared the following.

Almost all human beings use words to communicate because they have mostly forgotten other ways of communication, such as telepathy. Most humans have also forgotten to combine listening with feeling. Every word has a different feeling when used within a different context and different emotional setting. The Sidhe often repeat concepts that are important to understand on deeper levels. What you call repetition makes it possible for us to feel and experience many aspects of the concept that we are talking about. Therefore, we do not see it as repetition but as different ways to experience the subject at an increasingly deep level.

We do not communicate from mind to mind. We communicate from being to being, feeling and exploring each other to make a deeper connection. What you call repetition might be boring for you, but for us, it is simply continuous exploration.

From our perspective, humans have quick minds that work in a very limited way. They seem to always look for new things, and they get bored easily. They quickly believe that they already know a subject; therefore, they are not open and are, in general, less sensitive to the subtle elements of a subject and to the subtle differences that exist. From our perspective, the subtle aspects are needed to allow the development of a new consciousness. You are familiar with your old consciousness that helps you function and survive in a world full of challenges. Your next step as a race is the development of a consciousness based on love and respect in which you connect more deeply with everything you encounter. We love to explore this new consciousness with you. If you would like to explore with us, you have to deal with our "repetition" until you understand that it is not repetition but rather a continuous exploration of complex concepts that have many energetic and emotional aspects. If you can understand this and can work with this, you have bridged a gap between our two races and have laid a foundation for a new consciousness.

I was very happy with this sharing. It helped me to better understand them and their way of communicating. I also felt that it might help the readers to better understand what is presented in this book. Having gone through the experience of communicating with them, I felt the truth of what they shared.

One of the pre-editors, my friend Kristina, shared with me her feelings about the idea that the Sidhe were repetitious. Her impression was so aligned with what the Sidhe shared that I include it here: "Although I recognize that the Sidhe's communication style includes repetition, I did not find it distracting or annoying. It felt to me like they were summarizing what they had learned/shared to move on to put into proper context what they were about to share. However, if others find this repetitive, I agree that an explanation in the introduction would be worthwhile, as you never aim to put off the reader. I find the Sidhe to be clear communicators, and I like their style of sharing. However, I recognize that it requires that the reader be in a certain space of peaceful, open resting to enjoy this style of communication. I think people who are good natural listeners will get a lot out of the Sidhe's style."

Kristina was right. Aside from reading the actual content, you will get the most out of the book and the sharing when you open yourself to the energies. In addition to Kristina, two of the other pre-editors also strongly felt the energies and transmissions of the Sidhe when they were reading the manuscript. The Sidhe offer an opportunity. It is up to the reader to connect with what is offered. That determines how deeply you will go into the experience of connecting with the Sidhe and how ready you are for change.

TRANSFORMING THE IDEA OF LIMITATION

We have a tendency to see beings of higher consciousness who live in oneness as beings of unlimited possibilities. Many people would like to go to higher dimensions to overcome the limitations of the world we live in. However, a choice on any level of consciousness means that there is limitation. When you choose one thing, you also choose to reject something else. Even when you would be living in a higher-dimensional state, for example, the seventh-dimensional consciousness, the fact that you are in that consciousness state means that you have chosen to limit yourself to the experience of being in that dimension. Only Source is unlimited. Because we are part of Source, we have unlimited possibilities; however, any choice will, by definition, be limiting.

We have chosen to come into a reality that we call our world, Mother Earth, Gaia. By coming here and incarnating into a human body, we have accepted a certain role, and we are asked to fulfill that role. We can choose to see that as a limitation. We can also choose to see it as an opportunity to explore the reality in which we have chosen to live. Then we can let go of the idea of limitation and transform it into the idea of unlimited possibilities to explore and express ourselves within the reality into which we have chosen to incarnate.

OUR ROLE WITHIN GAIA

In this book, you will regularly come across the belief that we human beings have made an agreement with Gaia to fulfill a role. This role is to help raise the vibration of Gaia's system as a whole so that planet Earth and all who live on her will ascend to a permanent higher-vibrational state and consciousness level. Many people believe that Gaia is a very powerful, independent being who can determine her own journey. The idea that humans could have such a role as raising the vibration of her system might seem to be arrogant and can even be seen as an insult to her power.

There is no doubt in my mind that Gaia can determine her own evolution, growth, and expansion. However, that does not mean that she cannot delegate certain aspects and tasks to beings who live within her system. In fact, every being who exists in her system has a role to fulfill even though we are unable to understand what that role is. Our role might seem big and have great responsibility. Yet, I believe that we as a species have agreed to fulfill this role while Gaia is in charge. We can clearly see this in the message she shares in chapter 2.

It is time to accept our role instead of denying it. We have the power to change this world for the highest good of everyone and everything. For example, we have the collective power to change weather simply through the state of our collective consciousness. In *Crystal Skulls: Expand Your Consciousness*, I have given references to books that, completely independent of each other, mention the power of our collective consciousness.[4] The effect of our collective consciousness on our world is also studied by the Heart Math Institute.[5] Let us take responsibility for our agreement and change our collective consciousness to help this world to raise its vibration.

A BEGINNING

This book feels to me like a beginning. It is a beginning of sharing new options, possibilities, and explorations that can all lead to a new consciousness and a new way of being. I am aware that a follow-up on most subjects is needed. Some of these subjects are already in the works, meaning that I am in the process of collecting data and will continue doing that.

The purpose of sharing these dialogues is to empower you and to help you to expand. If you read this book solely from the perspective of your mind, you will miss a lot. However, when you read it with an open heart, you can open many possibilities. When the Sidhe and I were communicating, they created a bubble of consciousness that made it possible to feel and experience each other and to communicate without any adverse effect on them, their world, or me. When you read the transmissions of the Sidhe with an open heart, you will enter this consciousness bubble. You will experience their energies, and it will help you to expand your consciousness instead of expanding information in your mind. Then the dialogues will optimally help you to grow toward a new consciousness that will change the world for the betterment of all that lives on this beautiful planet. That is what Gaia hopes for and expects as an outcome of our connection and dialogues with the Sidhe.

CHAPTER 1

MEETING THE SIDHE

In recent times, there have been many reports from people who feel that they have made contact with the Sidhe. Several of these contacts have led to inspiring books. It seems that the Sidhe have reason to connect more frequently with humans. This will become clear as you read this book.

I never would have expected that the Sidhe would make a deeper connection with me. I am used to having a more superficial connection, as I do with many beings who live outside the physical world as we know it. I had a general understanding of who the Sidhe were from reading about them. Although I found them fascinating, they were not more interesting than the dragons with which I have a deep connection. It seems, however, that a fascination with the Sidhe is common. They represent mystery, and many people love mystery. Other people feel a strong resonance with them.

The Sidhe are also known by other names, such as fairies, the faery people, or elves. They are not little fairies like Tinkerbelle in the Disney film *Peter Pan* or the fairies Doreen Virtue communicates with. They are tall, human-like beings. When I met the Sidhe, I realized that they were quite different from the beings described in fantasy stories. Many names and roles have been given to them to awaken people to fantasy. What they have in common with Tolkien's elves is their energy and regality.

My first meeting was with two Sidhe, a man and a woman, and I had no clue at the time that I would be able to communicate with them. I saw these two beings, and for whatever reason, I knew that they were representatives of the Sidhe. In this chapter, I will explain who the Sidhe are, how I met them, the foundation of our meeting, and the sharing that followed.

THE SIDHE AND WHO WE THINK THEY ARE

A year ago, I had never heard of the Sidhe. Once I heard and read about them, I was curious about the root of their name. While the term "Sidhe" is quite old, it is not very well known. It is a short form of *aes sidhe* (*ees shee*). The aes sidhe are a supernatural race in Irish and Scottish mythology. They are compared to fairies and elves. It is said that they live in an invisible world (possibly underground) that coexists with our own.

In the *Book of Invasions*,[1] the Sidhe world is described as a parallel world in which the aes sidhe walk among the living. In Irish, aes sidhe means "people of the mounds." In many Gaelic tales, the aes sidhe are different versions or descendants of the Tuatha Dé Danann (people of the Goddess Danu),[2] the deities and deified ancestors of Irish mythology. Some sources describe them as the survivors of the Tuatha Dé Danann, who retreated into the Otherworld after the Milesians defeated them. The Milesians were a human race, the Gaelics. As part of the terms of their surrender to the Milesians, the Tuatha Dé Danann agreed to retreat and dwell underground in the *sídhe* (modern Irish, *sí*; Scottish Gaelic, *sìth*; or Old Irish *síde* [singular, *síd*]), the hills or earthen mounds that dot the Irish landscape.[3]

The name "Sidhe" comes from the Irish language, but the most familiar name is elves, as in the tales of Tolkien and many other stories, fantasies, and books. I loved the comic books in the Netherlands that were called *Elfquest*.[4] The common understanding is that elves are human-like but are connected more directly with magic, and they possess magical powers.

HOW IT ALL BEGAN

I learned of the Sidhe for the first time through the work of David Spangler.[5] Like Spangler, I am interested in the subtle worlds and the beings who live in them. I found Spangler's stories about the Sidhe intriguing, but I did not feel a particular interest in connecting with them. However, we are often guided in unexpected directions. If you truly believe in guidance, you will always follow the signals.

In the spring of 2014, my wife, Jeanne, and a friend, Deborah, renewed my interest in Spangler's work. Shortly thereafter, in July, I hiked with my friend Daniel deep into a canyon of the red rocks around Sedona, Arizona, to an area that I had not visited before. We were looking for ruins of the Sinagua, the people who lived in the area around Sedona somewhere between AD 700 and AD 1425.

Suddenly, it felt as if we were walking through a kind of energy barrier into a different world. I do not mean that suddenly the world looked different; rather, it felt different for me. The effect was unexpected and powerful. I felt nauseated and found it difficult to continue hiking. Still, I had a compulsion to go on. Although it was a considerable effort for me, we continued. We came to a point where I felt that we had to climb up to the next ledge. On the ledge, I was guided to a place that I knew would help me understand what was going on. I sat down, more or less collapsing. It took awhile before I could focus on the energies of the place where we were sitting.

When I examined how the energies felt, I realized that they were vaguely familiar. I knew I had encountered them a few times in my life, but I could not immediately identify when and where. Exploring more deeply into the energies, I realized what they were. The knowledge did not arise because I remembered where I had previously encountered them. It was just one of those moments of suddenly knowing.

The energies were of the Sidhe. I was totally surprised. I did not know much about the Sidhe beyond stories and legends of Irish fairies and what I had read in David Spangler's book. What I felt was not the fairy energy as I knew it from my studies of the morphogenetic grids of fairies. This energy was fundamentally different. Then I remembered where I had encountered it before. It was many years ago, high up on a ledge in Boynton Canyon in the Sedona area and also in Chaco Canyon in New Mexico. Not knowing at the time who they were, I called them the White Robes. In those days, I was studying the grid lines of the White Robes, which are described in my book *Gifts of Mother Earth*.[6] During these studies, I saw images of people clad in white. At the time, I thought they were part of the grid I was studying, but now I know that the images were of the Sidhe. This explains my familiarity with the energies of the place where I was sitting. At that time, I was not yet as sensitive to their energies as I have become.

Image 1.1: The location of the first Sidhe morphogenetic grid vortex, Sedona, Arizona.

The place I was guided to is a vortex of the morphogenetic grid of the Sidhe (see image 1.1). The term "morphogenetic grids and lines" will be used in this book many times. Therefore, it needs some explanation. Every species that exists, whether visible or invisible to us, has to have a morphogenetic field and grid to exist. The morphogenetic field contains the information for the full potential of a species. This field is a coherent energy system that forms a layer around the earth. The morphogenetic grid is a set of lines that is connected to the surface of the earth and laid out in patterns. The lines of the grid contain that part of the information from the field (potential) where a species is actively working with it. It determines what a species looks like and how it behaves.

Between the field and the grid is a connection. This connection is called a vortex. Hence, a vortex is a place where it is possible to connect both with the field and its full potential and the grid that holds the expressed characteristics of a species. Therefore, the vortex of a morphogenetic grid is the best place to connect with a species.[7] It is a place where you can learn everything about a species if you are able to receive and translate the energies into an understanding.

Sitting in this vortex, I was not able to translate or understand anything. When I calmed down, I became aware that we were not alone. I saw two beings, a man and a woman, standing at my right side looking at us. I knew they were two Sidhe. The way they showed themselves to me was quite human-like although they were clearly not human. The way they were standing, their slender but strong builds, and especially their energy made it clear that they were human-like but not human. While in general I am able to communicate to some degree with beings I perceive, I was not able to communicate with these two beings. I felt that they were friendly, but they were keeping their distance. It felt as if they were checking me out.

Although I did not know the meaning of this experience, I was excited about meeting the Sidhe. We stared at each other, and that was all there was. Even though I might not immediately understand, I know that there is always a reason when invisible beings make themselves visible to me (my friend did not see them). It was clear that I had to wait and see whether there was going to be any follow-up.

About a week later, I met the same two beings again. This happened deep in another canyon in the Sedona area. This time, I felt their willingness to communicate. That was not easy. Their way of connecting is completely different from all of my experiences with other beings. Usually once the connection is made, it is fairly consistent throughout the interaction. However, that was not the case with these two Sidhe. It felt like being connected, being disconnected, being connected, being disconnected, and so forth. It did not feel pleasant — definitely not stimulating and rather irritating. Completely unexpectedly, I received a clear message.

The way your mind both consciously and subconsciously works is, for us, very uncomfortable. Your jumping mind may not have much effect in your world. However, when we connect with you, every thought that we receive from you becomes part of our thought pattern and affects us immediately. If we are not careful, it may even affect our whole world. We will explain later to you why our minds work that way and why thoughts have such a strong effect on our world. The difference in the way the minds of our two races work is something that we need to learn to work with.

I was excited. This was the first time I heard a message from them. I felt their willingness to connect and their concern. I realized that if I wanted to communicate with them, the first thing I needed to learn was to stay focused during the time we were connected. I also hoped that they would be able to learn to deal with my mind a bit better so that maybe we could meet each other halfway. I did not want the preparations for clear communications to take too long. The Sidhe had my attention, and I was very interested in making a deeper connection to share with them. I was unaware that others who had encountered the Sidhe had the same problem with their communication, so I wondered whether I was different or whether the Sidhe who lived in the Sedona area differed from those in other parts of the world. Anyway, I was full of good intentions to make the communications work.

Both of my contacts with the Sidhe took place in very remote, difficult-to-reach areas, and I wondered whether I needed to be in such places to contact them. I preferred to connect with them from my home, so I could make notes or type information in a computer. My wife, Jeanne, and I decided to see whether it was possible to do so when supported by a small group of people. To make a connection, I had made an essence of the energies from a Sidhe morphogenetic grid vortex. This essence was made by connecting the essence of water with the essence of the vortex guided by the intention to program the water to hold the essence of the vortex. Jeanne and I have become quite accomplished with this process, and we use these essences regularly in our weekly group meditations.

The result was very exciting. In our group meditations, we use a large

Image 1.2: The crystal skulls used by the author and his wife at a location of many meditations and workshops.

circle of crystal skulls (see image 1.2) to amplify the energies of the theme with which we are working. In this case, the circle amplified the energies of the Sidhe vortex essence. It felt as if we were sitting on the vortex itself. Everyone could feel the energies of the Sidhe.

I also felt a reaction from the Sidhe that I would describe as surprise. A couple of days later, I understood their response. I was meditating at home when I unexpectedly felt the presence of the two Sidhe I had met before. I could feel a certain discomfort. I focused as much as I could to stabilize my mind, and then I asked them what was going on. They explained.

Over time, many interactions between the Sidhe and humans have been established. In current times, these connections have increased. To make these interactions possible, the Sidhe often provide tools to help humans connect. Examples are the Sidhe cards that you are familiar with[8] and a glyph that was shown.[9] These tools have a double function. It helps you to connect with us, the Sidhe. The frequency of the symbols makes this connection easier.

For us, they function as a warning, something like somebody ringing the doorbell to announce their arrival. The ringing of the doorbell gives us the choice to not open the door or to prepare ourselves to make contact possible. However, your ability to connect with us through, what you call, the morphogenetic grid was a big surprise to us. For us, it felt as if you stepped suddenly through the front door, ending up in our living room. There was no warning, and we were not prepared.

The tools that we have given to humans through different contacts make it possible for us to have control over the connection and the choice to say yes or no in each moment. With your ability to connect through the morphogenetic grid, you are the one who is in control. That is very unsettling for us, and we needed time to learn to work with this in a way that does not affect our world too much.

It is not about right or wrong. It is about the fact that your mental and emotional systems have such a big effect on us that it makes it that we need to prepare. Approaching us without warning is too challenging for us in this phase of our interaction.

I was shocked. It was never my intention to invade their space. I work with many other beings, always using the morphogenetic grids. It always felt totally okay for me, and I never received any reaction that this approach was inappropriate. It became clear to me that the Sidhe are in many ways quite different and that I need to be more careful in my approach to them.

Every time I connected with the Sidhe energies, I was aware of the same two Sidhe. I never saw another Sidhe, not even in those areas where I knew there were Sidhe present. I wished to connect more deeply with these two Sidhe, especially since they seemed to be my connection with the Sidhe world and energies. I wished to obtain more information about them but still respect their privacy.

The next opportunity I had, I addressed them directly. I asked them who they were and how I could connect while respecting their privacy. Their answer was an important step forward in our connection.

> To give our names in our language is not possible. However, we can give you names that come close in meaning to our real names. These names will help you to connect with us.
>
> In the past weeks, we have been preparing ourselves and are more able to work with you, especially since you also have made some shifts. You are already aware that we are a female and a male Sidhe. Because of the way we connect, you perceive us as two beings, but when you listen to us during our telepathic communication, you will only hear one. It does not matter which of the two of us is "speaking" with you. It will always be as if the same person is speaking. Therefore, it does not matter which of the two of us you call. In fact, by calling one of us, you will always call both of us.
>
> My name is Sha-Ra-El, and my name is Ki-Ra-El. We are respectively the one you see as a woman and the one you see as a man. In your language, "El" means "in or from God." For us, it means "being connected to the highest consciousness possible." We are also very connected to the consciousness of the Sun. We would like to share with you more about our connection with the Sun in later interactions. That is why "Ra" is in the names we use with you. The third part in our names reflects a specific quality. "Sha" means peacefulness and harmony, and "Ki" is a word you are familiar with: It is life force. With this, we have introduced ourselves to you.
>
> By using our names, you will no longer find yourself in the middle of an area or of an energy that may feel as an intrusion into our privacy. We now believe that working with the morphogenetic grids can be very helpful in understanding each other's worlds. We prefer not to use it as a way of connecting but as a way of exploring each other's worlds. When we interact more with each other, it may become clearer how to do this. We have never worked with these grids directly, so we need to explore more of their function before we can make any commitment or statement.

I was very happy with the improvement within our interaction. It was wonderful to have a simple way to connect without me being intrusive. I felt ready and willing to embark on a journey with them. But before doing so, I needed to ask them one more question. I did not seek out a connection with the Sidhe. I actually never thought about it. From my perspective, they chose to arrive on my path — that is, they had chosen to contact me. In order to move forward, I needed to have an idea or a feeling about the purpose of our connection.

As I mentioned earlier, many people already have encountered the Sidhe. Is that not enough? Why did they wish to add me to the people with whom they were already working? The next time I had the opportunity to connect with ShaRaEl and KiRaEl, I asked them. They responded.

We are very aware of your questions, and we fully understand them. The connection needs to be completely voluntarily, and the fact that we have connected with you does not mean that there is any obligation. All the people the Sidhe have made a connection with are people we feel have the abilities and qualities that make a connection and collaboration with us possible and useful. The purpose of the collaboration is to help each other to fulfill the function that we originally came to fulfill on Earth.

We were initially one race that split up and went into two different directions. Neither one of these directions has brought us to a point where we are fulfilling our purpose. We connect with people whom we believe are able to understand that changes are needed. We believe that we can help each other to change in such a way that each of us will come into alignment with our true essences.

We believe that in our personal interactions, we (the two of us and you) are able to support this process on a personal and a collective level. We know that this is what you do with your work. This is also what we do with ours. We would like to collaborate and to support each other in this process.

I was deeply moved by their sharing. I felt the energy and love with which these thoughts were shared. I also felt their passion. I resonated strongly with what they said because I knew that they were right. Their passion was also my passion. I made the commitment to begin the journey with them, feeling that it could help me in my personal development.

My commitment has always been to share what I learn with all people who feel attracted to what I offer. At that moment, I made the decision that I would share what I receive from the Sidhe in one way or another. I still did not fully understand why they wanted to connect with me, but suddenly it did not matter anymore. I felt deep gratitude, knowing that I was to embark on an interesting and important journey, and I felt ready for it.

Based on these initial connections, I am able to summarize the situation: The journey of human beings has not led to the results that were planned. The journey of the Sidhe also has not lead to the results that were planned. Both races failed to fulfill the commitment they had made to Gaia — to raise the vibration of the system to such a level that ascension is possible. I felt that the Sidhe were proposing to create a new consciousness in which both the Sidhe and human beings could fulfill their common commitment. I felt strongly that I desired to be a cocreator of this new consciousness. I hope that many humans will share these aspirations.

CHAPTER 2

GETTING TO KNOW EACH OTHER

Although the connection between the two Sidhe and me made me very happy, I had many doubts. Was I really the right person to communicate with the Sidhe? Wasn't it rather arrogant to think that I could contribute to the creation of a new consciousness? I had no idea how this new consciousness would look. I began to understand that the first step was to work with those aspects of the consciousness of the Sidhe and the humans who would contribute to the creation of this new consciousness and to avoid those aspects that it would not support. I wondered who was able to know the differences and guide the process.

Additionally, we needed to extract information related to the fulfillment of our purpose from the morphogenetic field and integrate it into the collective system of both races. All of these mentioned qualities needed to be integrated into a new way of functioning that would allow those working with this new consciousness to fulfill the purpose for which the original humanoid race came to Earth. It seemed complicated, if not impossible.

GAIA'S WARNING TO HUMANITY

It may be worthwhile to share why I, with all my personal and general doubts, was willing to continue with this seemingly preposterous plan of creating a new consciousness. My study of the energies of Earth (in my book *Gifts of Mother Earth*[1]) has brought me into a deeper connection with Earth and all that lives on it. This connection is quite different from the one that I had as an ecologist. As soon as I was willing to go beyond the physical and include the subtle energies, my whole perception of the world we are living in changed.

I became aware that the world we live in is more complex than science is willing to describe or even accept. There are many layers of realities within the system that we can call Gaia, and all these layers are occupied by subtle beings. The most important characteristic for me was that all of these worlds were different aspects of one consciousness — that of the being we call Gaia. During my second meeting with the Sidhe in a remote canyon (see image 2.1), I also made a powerful connection with Gaia. I do not believe in coincidences but in synchronicities, so I knew that there was a link between these two experiences.

Shortly thereafter, I received a message from Gaia. This message set a lot into motion within me. I am sharing this message here because it is most relevant to my willingness to work with the Sidhe.

I speak to you and to anyone who is willing to listen because I would like to give a message to humankind. This message has been given many times in different ways and in different forms. However, it seems that although people might hear the message, they are not or are barely responding to it, let alone acting on it. Therefore, this message will be repeated until there is a sufficient response.

When human beings became part of my system and souls wanted to incarnate in human-like bodies, an agreement was made. Earth would be a place to experience physicality and to learn how to create within a physical world. Humans were supposed to cocreate in such a way that it would lead to an increase in vibration of my physical expression. This would lead to the ascension of the physical system as a whole into higher states of consciousness. I, Gaia, would give my full support to this process. The possibility for this process is already built into my system. The incarnated souls, being the cocreators that they agreed to be, were the ones to manifest and complete this process.

Needless to say, humanity as a whole has failed to fulfill their part of the agreement. This is a consequence of the fact that human

Image 2.1: The location of our meeting with the Sidhe and Gaia, Sedona, Arizona.

beings no longer see themselves as part of the whole system. They see themselves as being above the system, and they see the system as something that is there for them to use and to take from as much as they think they need without love, respect, or giving something back. This has damaged the physical planet that is my body and nature, diminishing life within my system on a large scale.

The damage is reaching a point where I need to protect my system. That is why I am connecting with human beings who are willing to listen in order to tell them that this is a crucial time. Do you want to stay a part of my system? If that is the case, you need to take responsibility for your part of the agreement. See yourself again as part of the system that you call Gaia, and help each other to do so. Help each other to remember who you are and what you are here to do. All information is present within my system for those who are open to receive it.

This is an urgent message to ask you to please remember. Love again all that exists within my system: the stones, the crystals, the plants, the animals, and the many invisible beings. Through love, you will again find ways to work together with all your relatives and fulfill your purpose as a species. There is still time. However, be aware: Time is running out!

Although this message was given in love, it was also a wake-up call. What were we going to do about our role and function in this world?

HUMANS' RELATIONSHIP WITH THE SIDHE

Through my connection with the Sidhe, I felt that they had a similar awareness. I realized that the Sidhe were aware that they were also caught up in their own creation of reality and had not fulfilled the role they were supposed to play. I had no clue why the Sidhe had a similar awareness because, in all honesty, I still had no clear picture of the Sidhe and who they were. We, humans and Sidhe, are children of Gaia. But what is our relationship? So I asked my new Sidhe friends, ShaRaEl and KiRaEl, about their vision of our relationship.

At this moment, the Sidhe and humans are far apart in almost every way. Although you can say that we are related races, the difference has become so big that we can almost be seen as two different species. However, this has not always been the case. According to those of our race who are the wisdom and record keepers, there was a time in which our two races were one. We are the star beings who came to Earth a long time ago. Yes, you are hearing this correctly. According to our stories, human beings and Sidhe share the same ancestors who came from the stars. Your race also has knowledge that can confirm this.

We invite you to look at the morphogenetic information. You differentiate between morphogenetic fields and morphogenetic grids. This is knowledge that was no longer active in our collective mind, but you made us remember. You have defined a morphogenetic grid as the energies and information from the morphogenetic field with which a species is working actively. As you have discovered, the morphogenetic grids of our two races are different. However, the morphogenetic field that we are connected with is the same for both races. This means that our races have taken different aspects out of the potential for our species.

The Sidhe started to work with aspects of the potential that was different from the aspects with which you were working, and consequently, our consciousness began to separate. We began to create two different races with two different morphogenetic grids. However, we still have the same potential.

When our common ancestors came to Earth, their basic purpose was to explore the physical reality and become cocreators in such a way that the overall vibrational state of this physical world would be raised. What the Sidhe did was to raise the vibration of the reality they chose to create. But that did not include Gaia as a whole. We disconnected ourselves from those who had chosen to connect more deeply with physical matter so that we could stay in a higher vibrational state. Those who chose to connect more deeply with the material world became caught in an increasing physical density and as a race were decreasing their vibration. In different ways, we both lost our ability to connect with the whole and therefore could not fulfill our purpose as per the agreement with Gaia.

In this phase of our evolution, both the Sidhe and humans are caught in their own realities. We are both afraid to step out of our realities, even though somewhere we know that they are supposed to be more than what we experience. There exists a blueprint of who we are supposed to be. That blueprint is the morphogenetic field of both of our species. That is why we need to help each other overcome the tendency to lock ourselves within the reality of our grids and to create a consciousness that uses the gifts of both races, connecting with the morphogenetic field to create something new that will allow us to fulfill our agreement.

Although much of what they shared was more or less familiar and completely in line with my own thoughts and ideas, it was good to hear it from beings I originally thought were superior to us. Having studied the morphogenetic grids and field to the degree I have (and having published information about them in *Gifts of Mother Earth*)[2], it was quite a realization that the Sidhe shared the same morphogenetic field with us. That means we are like one species with two different expressions. This could explain the reason the Sidhe are seeking contact and connecting with us. We both hold a part of the expression of our species.

EXPLORING THE IDEA OF ONENESS

Both the race called the Sidhe and that called humans are locked in the way they are using a part of the morphogenetic field. We truly need a new consciousness from those of both races who are willing to tap into the fullness of the morphogenetic field. The implication might be that we need to create a new humanoid race. The decision to connect with this new consciousness could create a new race of human-like beings that might have characteristics of both the Sidhe and the human races.

I am very aware that for most people, this is all rather far-fetched. I wondered how this was for the Sidhe race, so I asked my new friends.

The Sidhe are not a homogenous race. Similar to humans, there are several sub-races. Each sub-race has its own uniqueness and its own expressions, much like what you see in your world. We are more flexible, and we will talk about that in a later exchange, but even within this seeming flexibility, we are also stuck in our beliefs. These beliefs make it impossible for many Sidhe to connect with humans. They see humans as a permanent threat to our way of living. Although the two worlds are quite separate, as we will see later, these worlds do interact with each other, and the human emotional energies — especially those of fear, anger, and aggression — are a permanent threat to our reality. Therefore, most Sidhe would prefer more distance and barriers between our races and definitely are not open to a connection between us. They fear that the connections some of us have made have already influenced the Sidhe race in a negative way. Similar to your reality, we will never get everyone to agree to the connection and collaboration with humans.

For us, freedom is paramount. So no one will force anyone to go in a direction they do not want. Therefore, all Sidhe who connect with humans do that voluntarily based on the belief that it is essential to do so. We believe that from the human side, the same needs to be true. We like to work only with those humans who have chosen freely to connect or collaborate with us.

What we feel is that within both races, there are two groups. The first group consists of beings who lay the foundation for a connection. They receive information, and they are invited to study and explore this information. The second group will be those who feel called to help in studying the material that is shared and to contribute in this way. They may not have a direct connection but feel a connection with the general goal: the fulfillment of the purpose of our essences, which is the intent we had set collectively when we entered Gaia and is still valid.

I loved the sharing of my Sidhe friends because I strongly resonated with what they expressed. It felt as if I were connecting with longtime friends who have shared so much that we think alike in many ways but have and hold our own uniquenesses. My initial resistance and doubts were melting away more and more every time I talked with them.

Many years ago, I had reserved the domain name TheWeAreOneProject .com with the intention of creating a website that would help raise the world's consciousness of Oneness. At this point in my conversation with the Sidhe, I realized the project and what we were communicating about now were along the same lines. I had been on the right track.[3] Initially, I felt the same when I realized what this new consciousness was about. However, whenever I connected with the two Sidhe, I immediately felt more confident. This was not something I had to figure out on my own. This was a process in which we could help and support each other. I did not have to know what the result might look like. I simply had to start the journey. Then I realized that the journey had already started. I just had to continue one step at a time.

TO BE ABLE TO LIVE AMONG THE SIDHE

I felt that there was one question that I needed to ask before processing all that had happened and had been discussed. I encountered the Sidhe energy in a certain area north of Sedona. I felt them there, but I did not see anything. I could "see" my two friends but nothing else. I wondered whether I really had entered into one of the areas they lived in and how it was possible that the Sidhe were living in a place where I could not see or feel anything more than a strong energy field. Can I only see what they allow me to see? When I asked these questions, I felt more distance, similar to what I felt in the beginning. I immediately told them that I did not expect a full answer but possibly something more general. I also mentioned that there was no need to answer my question if they did not wish to do so.

Do not interpret our reaction in the wrong way. The hesitation you felt was not so much from us. There is one aspect that we have not yet shared with you. Although there is complete freedom for everyone to follow what he or she chooses, there is one exception. The agreement is that we stay in telepathic connection with the community, especially when it involves issues that concern the whole community.

Individually, a Sidhe may not agree with what another Sidhe does. However, no one has the right to take others from their chosen paths. There is one exception: when it is felt by the community that what an individual is doing is dangerous for the community as a whole. Sharing with you in this manner is not considered dangerous. That becomes different when you talk about the places where we live and how we live.

In general, we have withdrawn into remote areas or the underground. With the human tendency to continually expand, many places that once were our homes had to be abandoned. Most of our race went underground when their places were invaded in such a way that it became impossible to keep the effects of human thoughts and emotions out of our world. There are factions of Sidhe who would love to live with humans in the same area, but at this time, that is still impossible.

You are already aware of parts, mainly the edges — of the area seen from your physical perspective — that we are still living in. When I say "we," I'm talking about the community of which we are a part. You can see us as a separate tribe within the Sidhe race. Because we are telepathic, we share with other tribes, but we cocreate with our own community, using the unique qualities of the Sidhe that are part of our tribe. This allows our community to look different from any other community. That is quite different from the creation of your world in which many towns look similar. For us, that is unthinkable.

In later communications, we would like to share more about how we create our community. Realize that all we can do, you can potentially do as well. And the same is true the other way around. You may not be aware, but you have gifts to give us. We will also talk about that later.

Fortunately, the area we live in is quite inaccessible for most human beings. Those who reach the area we live in are in a state in which there is not much negative interference with us. We hope that this situation can be maintained as long as possible; therefore, we prefer not to say much more.

Their explanation helped me to understand their reaction better. Through my connections with them, I appreciate that our presence is a threat to the way their system works. The creation of a new consciousness could make it possible for the Sidhe and humans to live together in peace and harmony, at least in some areas.

It would be wonderful if the Sidhe could live in such a way that instead of feeling as if they need to avoid us, we would be able to enjoy each other's company. Such a development would finally create the possibility of working together to fulfill the purpose of our combined races. I can imagine Gaia's joy when this happens. It is up to us to make it happen.

CHAPTER 3

OUR ORIGINS AND THE INFLUENCE OF THE STARS

According to the Sidhe, the common origin of our races is the most important subject with which to start our sharing. Of course, this information about the origins of our races depends wholly on the Sidhe's memories. Through their sharing, it may be possible for us to feel once again the connection that exists between our two races. The Sidhe also believe that it may open the possibility for every human to explore the connections that exist with the different star systems and their personal place of origin. In this way, each person, as well as the human race as a whole, can better understand who he or she truly is.

I liked the idea of reconnecting with our origins and the star systems with which we might have a connection. This is an exciting personal subject for me, because I have done much research on the relationship of human beings with the different star nations. Some of the research results were summarized in *Crystal Skulls: Expand Your Consciousness*.[1] I studied the star ancestors mainly through crystal skulls and also through portals (for portals, see *Gifts of Mother Earth*[2]).

Therefore, I was most curious what the Sidhe would say about this subject. I was expecting them to start with a sharing when, to my surprise, they asked me first to give a short summary of my discoveries. In their opinion, this approach was a true sharing and dialogue. Additionally, it would help them to share the aspects that are mutually relevant. With some reluctance, I agreed.

THE RELATIONSHIP BETWEEN HUMANS AND STAR NATIONS

My first interest in star nations and star systems was induced by my crystal skull research. The legend of the crystal skulls states that there are twelve star nations that have given information to the people of Earth. Once the people of Earth are able to integrate this information from the twelve star systems into one coherent understanding, there will be a shift in consciousness. I always believed that the "people of Earth" meant humans. However, given the presence of the Sidhe and our relationship with them, I began to realize the Sidhe are a part of the people of Earth and have something to contribute to this shift as well.

My second line of interest came through my studies of Earth energies. About fifteen years ago, I found vortexes that were completely different from the ones I had been studying. These vortexes connect Earth to places and dimensions outside of Earth somewhere out in the universe. These types of vortexes are called portals. While vortexes function within the Earth system, portals connect Earth to something outside of its system. This may be other planets or stars or could also be other dimensions.

Initially, I had no idea where these portals connected. I could feel that different portals had different energies, but that was as far as I could go. Over time, I began to recognize energies, knowing that I had felt them before. Slowly, patterns began to emerge. The next step was to find the names of the star systems or other places in the universe to which these different portals connected. With the support of others, I began to define different portals. As more time passed, I was able to define more energies of star systems. However, I am acutely aware that I am only at the beginning of my understanding of the many different star systems with which we are connected.

During my research, I discovered two main types of portals: One group had energy lines that connected them with other portals that had the same energy. However, the majority of portals I found did not have such connecting lines. This means that these portals were not connected with each other in a way that I can currently detect. The portals with energy lines that connect with each other seem to be the portals that human beings use more. I say this with some caution because there is much that I do not know or understand. Understanding portals and their energies is like learning a complex language:

I am glad that I can recognize words and some sentences, but I am far from fluent.

Throughout time, indigenous people have connected frequently with portals found in ruins of structures that they have built. Most of my research on portals and their relationship to indigenous people has been done in the American Southwest, primarily in the Sedona area, and this research continues. The Sinagua culture had a deep connection with star nations. I have written much about their connections with the star nations, whom they called their ancestors, in *Crystal Skulls: Expand Your Consciousness*.[3] New research has added a lot more information.

In the Sedona area, there are several canyons that have ledges on rock walls with many small ruins, often only consisting of one room, that are built around a portal. After a while, I realized that some of these ruins were connected with each other in different ways. It seems some of these portals were created a long time ago by a consciousness unknown to me, and other portals were created later. I call the earlier type primary portals, and their creators are unknown to me. I call the later type secondary portals. These were created through collaboration between people of Earth and the star people. This means that there was interaction on both sides. I do not know how often these kinds of collaborations occurred, but it is possible that they are more frequent than we think.

HUMAN ORIGIN

During my first two visits to the Sidhe area, I found portals that were rather new to me. The most common portals (the ones with connecting lines) connect to the Pleiades, Sirius, Arcturus, Orion, Alpha Centauri, Andromeda, and Cygnus. While I was in the Sidhe area, I found a portal to Ursa Major, Antares, Pegasus, and an unknown star system. Although I have found portals to Ursa Major before, Antares and Pegasus were new to me.

When I tuned into the star system connected with the unknown portal, I heard Spica. I had never heard about Spica before. From Internet research, I learned that Spica is the brightest star in the constellation of Virgo. The interesting aspect of these four portals was that I could feel that the Sidhe had used all of them. More interesting was the observation that a portal to Sirius in the same area did not give me a feeling that the Sidhe used it, even though it was very close (less than thirty yards) from the portal to Spica. I found this interesting because Sirius is a star system with which the human race is very connected.

Many people believe that they originate from Sirius. Dolphins and whales are believed to come from Sirius, and there was a strong connection with Sirius during the Egyptian culture. All these observations raised many questions for the Sidhe.

My first question was related to our origin. If we were initially one people, then wouldn't that imply we have the same origin? As the Sidhe remember more about our ancestry than we do, their memories could help us to reestablish our connection with our essence. The Sidhe then shared the following.

Over time, we too lost a great deal of information about our origins. Those among us who are the keepers of our history will tell you that we originate from the stars. We are aware that this is vague from your perspective. We will try to share something about our connection with star systems that we feel is relevant for our understanding of the races.

One of the challenges we have is that our two races have different ways of looking at the stars. We also notice that your knowledge about the different star systems is very limited, even though you might know more than the average person about this subject. Therefore, we will not be able to provide the information that we would like to share. There simply is not a reference system within you to do so, at least not presently.

Before we can continue, we have to separate both the Sidhe and the human beings into two main groups. The first main group is the group of the original souls. The second group is composed of different waves of souls who came to Earth to join either the Sidhe or the human race. This may seem irrelevant for the story of our origin, but it is not. Let us explain this in more detail.

The first wave comprised the original group of the ancestors of both the Sidhe and the humans. To some degree, their origins are still known to us. They came from many different star systems. The idea was to have as much variation as possible within the group of souls that came to Earth to ensure the success of settling on Earth and experiencing a physical world.

According to our keepers of history, these first souls were aware that souls had never experienced physicality. While Earth was receiving souls, many other souls went to other star systems. This was the beginning phase of humanoid races in the universe. Most of the souls went into this galaxy, which you call the Milky Way, while other souls went into other galaxies, mainly the ones you call Andromeda and Triangulum.

The consequence is that there is not one star system that can be indicated as *the* origin of both races. It became even more complicated when other souls incarnated into the different humanoid races in this galaxy. Therefore there are more relationships than the one between our two races: All humanoid races throughout the universe are related, hence the importance of remembering that we are one humanoid superspecies.

Human beings especially tend to identify differences and then make judgments based on preferences. We are not saying that we are free of judging, but we have more understanding and live harmoniously with the realization that we are all one.

The waves of souls that came to Earth later often came from different areas within this galaxy where they already had incarnational experiences. They already had some experience living in a physical reality or living within the consciousness of a star or a planet. Based on their experiences, they chose to join one of the two races on Earth that were developing: the Sidhe or the humans. This choice strengthened the separation between the two races.

The souls that joined either the Sidhe or the humans often came from different parts of the galaxy or even from other galaxies. Coming from different parts of the universe or even from within the galaxy requires different doorways to enter Earth. Due to the increasing differences between the souls who joined one of the two races, the major doorways that were used to reach Earth differed based on whether they chose to join the Sidhe or the humans. This is the origin of the stories of remembering the areas that were used as way stations on the path to Earth. While we were already separated, the separation became even stronger.

Many of your aboriginal cultures and an increasing number of people from your modern times say that they remember coming from the Pleiades or Sirius. These are the two most commonly named star systems among the human race. The Pleiades and Sirius are two major galactic doorways that souls need to go through before they enter into this world (Earth). These doorways are also way stations where souls are prepared before entering Earth. These doorways and way stations are used mainly by the souls who join the human race and not by souls who join the Sidhe. The Sidhe increasingly avoided connecting with the Pleiades and Sirius because these systems were associated with the human race.

Later, waves of souls who joined the Sidhe began to use other doorways to enter the reality of the Sidhe. These doorways are connected with Arcturus and Alpha Centauri. This does not mean that humans who have a connection with Arcturus or Alpha Centauri came through these doorways and as a consequence have a Sidhe connection. We are very aware that there are many humans who have a strong connection with these star systems. However, having a connection with these star systems does not mean that they used the doorways connected with them. Most likely, they still used the doorways of Sirius and Pleiades. However, a connection with Arcturus or Alpha Centauri could be a way to bring us closer together.

My feeling was that this last comment was directed to me personally. I feel a powerful connection with Arcturus, and I have spent a lot of time studying the portals to it. Although I feel a strong connection with the Sidhe, I do not feel that my connection with Arcturus makes me more related to them.

At that point, I needed a break. I noticed that their story was not merely a story. I felt that when they shared, I was a part of the story. This was distinctly different from feeling the energy of the story: I felt more like a participant rather than an observer. This is not easy to explain, but it is definitely different from channeling. The telepathic transmissions of the Sidhe felt more like a participation in their thoughts.

INTERACTING WITH STAR SYSTEMS

It took a couple days to reconnect. Meanwhile, I had been pondering over what was shared. I realized that the deeper truth was that the origin of the first wave of souls had been lost in time. David Spangler also refers to the orientation of the Sidhe toward the stars.[4] While there is no doubt that they have this connection, there is a lot to learn about the different star systems with which the Sidhe and humans are connected. Each star system has unique energy patterns and frequencies. With which star systems are the Sidhe connected? Are we connected with star systems different from the Sidhe?

Based on our earlier conversations and those observations I had made while in the Sidhe area, it seemed that their connection with the star systems was quite different from ours, both with respect to importance as well as to the systems with which they connected. As mentioned, I had observed that many peoples all over the world have a connection with particular star systems. Also, many people on their spiritual paths have a connection with one or more star systems.

I asked the Sidhe whether it is truly helpful to analyze the connection our two races have with star systems given all of these differences, especially in light of the idea of developing a new consciousness. I also asked this because I was no longer certain that analyzing star systems was an important topic to proceed with.

The short answer to the question is yes, it is important to look at our connections with star systems. However, we would like to give a longer answer to explain why we feel this way. We are aware that the importance of connecting with the stars may seem to be more important for the Sidhe than for humans. However, we believe that this is only partly true.

The main difference may be in the way we work with the stars. We say this because we are aware that many people like to look at the stars, often with a strange, difficult-to-explain longing. In addition, your astrology, which is quite popular in your world, is based on the influence of stars and planets. It becomes more common in your world to define yourself and others based on the star system the Sun was in at the moment of your birth.

Looking at the stars at the moment of birth and their meaning is not only happening in your world but also in ours. We have a system quite similar to your astrology. We also believe that the moment of birth is important because of the energies present in that moment. We believe that the soul actually influences the time of birth to create the most optimal conditions for the newborn to succeed in its life's mission.

Our knowledge of the energies of the stars is, however, much more developed. We are in no way criticizing your astrology; to the contrary. We believe that it is one of the reasons that we may be able to create a new consciousness.

You are aware of your interaction with the energies of planetary and star systems, and that is important for the expansion of your energies and helps raise them to higher levels. What we mean by the statement that our form of astrology is "more highly developed" is that we have not lost as much of the knowledge and understanding of the energies of the stars and planets as you have. While you entered denser vibrations, the ability to connect and understand the energies of the stars diminished.

Our decision to stay in a more etheric state allowed us to maintain a deeper connection and a deeper understanding of the energies from all bodies outside the planet we live on. Understanding these energies makes it easier to remember your true essence. Once you remember your true essence, it will also be easier to connect with the energies of the different star systems.

When we look at the star energies, we need to look at two aspects. Astrology, to use your word, mainly focuses on the energies at the time of either conception or birth. We believe that both aspects are important. While most humans do not know when their conceptions took place, they are at least, to some degree, aware when they were born, even when it may not be possible to give the exact moment of birth. The energies at the moment of birth have a powerful influence on the makeup of the personality and on the journey of life. However, the soul has its own star connections, an important awareness that humans have forgotten and one that is of particular importance to the Sidhe.

We have Sidhe who specialize in helping us to connect or reconnect with the star energies that resonate with our souls who say that the Sidhe are more connected to the stars. We refer to the soul's resonance with a star system "connecting with your essence."

I loved the clarity of this information. Within small groups, we have explored which star system resonated most strongly with our physical systems and our souls. We limited this exploration to the twelve star systems that were connected to crystal skulls. Our explorations were facilitated by the crystal skull setup in our home, whereby all of the crystal skulls had been grouped based on their resonance with the twelve star systems (refer to image 1.2 in chapter 1). Without the availability of these crystal skull energies, I would not have known how to proceed.

Since then, I have visited many portals to many different systems even beyond the star systems that are connected to crystal skulls. Interestingly, these journeys have not changed the conclusions I came to many years ago.

CONNECT WITH THE STAR ENERGIES OF THE SOUL

My physical system and ways of functioning seem to resonate with the energies of Sirius while my soul seems to have a strong resonance with Arcturus. I wondered whether the Sidhe were undertaking similar research. My Sidhe friends confirmed as much and added more information.

In principle, we have a similar process. However, the depth with which we look at the energies is different from what you describe. We do not disagree with the conclusions that you have drawn, but there is more to it. This has to do with your definition of "soul."

When you looked at the resonance of the soul with a star system, you looked at only a part of the total being that you are. The term "soul fragment" comes closest to the part that you looked at. In a sense, you can also use the term "high self," as far as we understand the use of that term in your world.

We see the soul as a larger entity that has its own journey through different expressions. If we want to understand who you truly are, we need to connect to that larger aspect — what we call the soul. When you look at the larger being that you are, you may find a different star system, assuming you are able to define that star system. Looking at that star system will be a part of reconnecting with your true essence.

Before closing the subject of star systems, we wish to share more about our perspective. Like you, or at least like some of you, we look at the stars at the moment of conception and birth. That helps us to understand the gifts and challenges that we might face in our lifetimes. Because we live so much longer than you do, the knowledge of these energies and how they affect us is of prime importance to us. In addition, we give a lot of attention to defining the soul vibrations.

With what star system does the soul resonate? Although many assume that the star system a soul resonates with is also its place of origin, there are many others who say that this is not necessarily true. However, studying the systems with which our souls resonate helps us to understand more about ourselves and helps us to awaken more of our potential. This ideology is an important aspect of our culture.

We believe that this ideology is equally important for human beings. For you personally, understanding the connection between your higher self and Arcturus is helpful. Reflecting more deeply about expanded aspects of yourself that we call soul will facilitate your understanding of your true essence and the gifts that you possess to offer to Gaia.

This information was very helpful to me, as it created much clarity. However, from another perspective, it was frustrating. I thought I knew which star system my soul resonated with, and now that knowledge disappeared. I asked how I could identify the star system my soul resonated with. I was sure many people would like to know that as well. What system do the Sidhe use? There was silence for a long time. I doubted my question as the connection was reestablished.

The delay in response has nothing to do with a lack of willingness to answer your question. The difficulty in answering this question is that we do not have such a system that we can describe in simple terms.

There are two reasons for that. The first one is that there are many star systems that we do not know how to describe to you. The second is that the way we work with energies and the way our thought processes work are too different from yours to communicate this properly.

As important as the question is and as much as we would like to give you an answer, within the possibilities of our current connection, this is not yet possible. We are very happy that we are able to share this much. Maybe we can come back to this subject when the connections have deepened and the way to transfer information has expanded. We feel, however, that we need to end our sharing about star systems for now and start exploring other subjects.

I experienced a glimpse of the big differences in the ways we functioned. The apparent ease with which the sharing had flowed led me to forget that I was communicating with a race that was markedly different from us in so many ways. I reminded myself to remember these significant differences between us and, more importantly, to not set up expectations that were not real.

MEDITATION TO CONNECT WITH THE ENERGIES OF THE STAR SYSTEM OF YOUR SOUL

The question of how to connect with star energies related to the soul kept circling in my mind. My Sidhe friends suggested that we could adapt a meditation that I use often. I wondered about the value of a meditation, given that we do not have a reference point to define these star energies in understandable terms. The Sidhe had a clear answer.

You may not have fully understood the importance of connecting with the star energies of your soul. It is not important to know what name to give these energies or to know where they originally come from. It is about making the connection and awakening the energies of your soul in a way that you as a physical being begin to connect and resonate with. This is an important way to connect with your essence and to raise your vibration. It is what you call "beginning to remember who you are."

The purpose of this is to connect and strengthen the key energies of your soul thereby allowing it to awaken your whole being. You do not need to know the name of a star system to accomplish such an awakening.

I thanked them from my heart. I realized that I always tend to need to know before I can fully work with something. They are right; it is about the connection and the deepening of that connection. The following meditation will help you to make and deepen such a connection.

- *Close your eyes, and make yourself as comfortable as possible.*
- *Take a few deep breaths, and begin to relax. Focus on your breathing to relax more deeply.*
- *Just relax; go deeper and deeper. Allow yourself to sink as deeply as possible into the here and now. Nothing else matters but relaxing as deeply as you can.*
- *Bring your awareness to the center of your heart, the location of your divine essence. Imagine this essence as a sphere of white light. Allow this white light to shine throughout your physical system. Let it shine into every corner, every cell, awakening and increasing the vibration of your whole system.*
- *Feel how this white light holds unconditional love that is now spreading throughout your entire physical system. This love is meant for you, inviting you to unconditionally love and accept yourself exactly as you are now.*
- *Now set the intention to connect with the essence of your soul, that higher aspect of you that goes beyond your high self. Invite the energy of the star system your soul resonates with. Allow these energies to permeate your whole system. Trust that you have made the connection, and surrender to the flow.*
- *Feel gratitude for the gifts that these energies bring to you. Recognize and know that these energies are part of your essence. They help you to begin to remember who you truly are.*
- *Sit in this energy for as long as you feel comfortable. Know that you will never feel the same as you did before. You now are more of who you truly are.*
- *When you feel ready, take a deep breath, become aware of your physical body — your feet or butt on the ground or chair — and slowly open your eyes again.*

There is no doubt in my mind that this meditation, when done regularly, will help you to connect to the star system your soul resonates with and to the essence of who you truly are. This practice is an important step in the cocreation of this new consciousness!

CHAPTER 4

THE SEPARATION

O nce upon a time, we were one species and one race. It is clear, given that we are so far apart now, that we had formed two different races, if not two different species, as a result of some type of separation. I have also read about such a separation in other books. In my connection with the Sidhe, I began to feel this separation and the many differences it has caused.

Although it seemed that the communication with the Sidhe was easy, it was actually a process of continually searching for ways to be understandable to each other. I felt and realized that there were many aspects in the ways we think and perceive reality that are very far apart. However, these differences also created a compelling invitation to explore each other's worlds, thereby learning all that we could in order to find ways to create a new consciousness that could bring together the positive aspects of both worlds. These types of thoughts kept me engaged. They helped me to accept that we were limited in some areas and that we had to wait for expansion or changes from both sides to facilitate further sharing.

THE SEPARATION BETWEEN THE SIDHE AND HUMANS

Each communication between the Sidhe and humans will have different challenges; therefore, what is communicated will differ. I wanted to hear from ShaRaEl and KiRaEl what they knew about the process of separation. I also wanted to hear their perspectives on the consequences of this separation of our races. By that point, I was aware that within the Sidhe world, there are also different points of view. For me, the most important aspect in understanding the differences is to know the next step: What are our similarities, and how can we use them for further explorations? When I asked my Sidhe friends to share about the separation, I could feel something that I interpreted as resistance, and I wondered about the source.

Among those of us who are reaching out to connect with humans, the history of the separation is not a favorite subject. This is not because we feel that there is anybody to blame for this separation. The history of the separation makes us aware that the original race that we both descended from, the Founders race as we call them, had actually failed in its mission. Let us start with the mission as we know it. We are aware that our contact has brought up some ideas about the mission as well. [They are referring to the information from Gaia in chapter 2.]

As has been shared by those who are the keepers of our history, the first group of souls came to Earth millions of years ago. They were the ones who learned how to create with the information that was provided by the consciousness of Gaia and that was available in what you call the morphogenetic field. They also created in collaboration with Gaia the bodies that were used by the souls to explore this world. These bodies were modeled from a matrix that can be called the humanoid matrix of the universe (of which Gaia is a part) but adjusted to the specific matrix [meaning morphogenetic field] of Gaia.

These bodies were not entirely solid. They were malleable energy forms that to a certain degree could change their density, but they were never as solid as the physical body of Gaia. The entrance of the first wave of souls into Gaia's system happened with the total support of Gaia. The agreement was that this new species would use its ability to connect with higher vibrational systems to bring higher-frequency energies into the physical system of Earth to raise the vibration to such a level that ascension, as you would call it nowadays, would be possible.

Although we are talking about the physical body of Earth, we were aware of and include the many subtle layers. You are beginning to become aware again of these subtle layers and the many subtle beings that live within them. It is even difficult for us, the Sidhe, to understand the world of our ancestors, let alone expect you to understand it. You would call it a paradise because then there was harmony among the different vibrational worlds and all who lived in these worlds. Most of these worlds still exist, and some of them have changed little.

In order for the Founders race to raise the physical vibrations of this world, they needed to connect with those physical aspects. Herein lies the root of the separation. In the attempt to connect with the physical aspects, a loss of the fluidity and the higher vibrations began. Many of the Founders realized that in order to truly connect with the physical reality, they needed to lower the vibration of their bodies. Soon it was realized that there was less freedom of movement, less ability to create, and possibly a loss of awareness of who they were.

The first signs were obvious. There was a faction that was not willing to continue, and this faction grew rapidly in size. They felt that there were other ways to fulfill the agreement made with Gaia. The remaining Founders wanted to continue with the process of making a deeper connection with the physical world. In that phase, the Founders race totally respected the choices that each individual would like to make. So the beginning of separation became a fact.

Maybe this could have worked out for both factions if the ones that wanted to maintain their high vibrational states had not grown increasingly worried about the possibility that they might be sucked into the energy of what was called densification. They started searching for ways to protect themselves so as to prevent a descent into matter and a loss of many of the qualities that were so highly favored by the ancestors of the Sidhe.

As part of their actions, they created a world of higher vibrations that began to separate more fully from the physical world. In that process, they pulled the higher vibration into their world to create the world they desired without realizing that this actually stimulated the densification of those who were connecting with the physical world. It would have been possible to access these higher vibrations from the Infinite Source, but they were so much a part of this world that they believed that they had to access the vibrations from this world.

Consequently, they contributed to a stronger separation and a quicker densification process for the human race. It is this aspect that gives the feeling of discomfort in many of the Sidhe who wish to cocreate the new consciousness with humans. We are well aware that the actions of our ancestors had accelerated the separation and that they were the probable cause of the lack of fulfillment of the agreement with Gaia.

In our history, it is not clear what or who induced the next phase. However, what happened was that more souls came to Earth. We also do not know how the souls chose either Sidhe or human ancestors. The general belief is that this second wave of souls was supposed to prevent further separation. The current situation indicates that they were not successful. The separation accelerated and reached a point of no return.

Subsequent waves of souls could not bring true change. Humankind sank more deeply into matter to such a degree that it became dangerous for the Sidhe, and they withdrew even further from the human race. The human race was genetically modified many times by different extraterrestrial races, both in positive and negative ways, resulting in who you are now. This increased the separation even more.

Although I had heard or read aspects of this story from others, it is a considerably different experience to receive the information telepathically and to feel the energies accompanying it. The experience raised many questions, but I felt that it was inappropriate to ask them then or perhaps ever.

I wondered why no faction tried a different approach, such as creating a new way of being in that world similar to what we are attempting now. There could have been a merger among members from both groups, the Sidhe and humans, who wanted to collaborate to find a different way from withdrawal (like the Sidhe) or diving into the physical (like humans). This was one of those moments that I could feel that we will not ever know what truly happened because the beings in those days were so different from who we are today.

The information shared by the Sidhe was the textbook version of the story. I felt that so much more had taken place in those days. After all, these beings functioned on a higher level of consciousness, and in the story, they seemed to me to be acting like a bunch of naïve teenagers. I believe that there is more to it than one group being afraid and one group being brave and stupid. Although looking at the offspring of the last group, maybe it did happen! Maybe the ones who went more deeply into physicality were naïve, innocent, and unaware of any consequences. There was no reference point providing clues about what might happen and the consequences. Maybe the whole process for the human faction was a childlike exploration, the purpose that fundamentally might have been to learn what it meant to be, live, and create in a physical world.

I could feel that while I was pondering these thoughts, the Sidhe withdrew. They did not enjoy this type of mental process. They were drawn easily into the energies of my musings, which were uncomfortable for them. Such discomfort could be the deeper reason for the growing differences and separation of our ancestors. When the human faction became denser, their thoughts influenced the Sidhe ancestors in increasingly uncomfortable ways. To protect their essence, they felt they had to withdraw.

The behavior of my Sidhe friends helped me to become more compassionate to the ancestors of both races. It also helped me to better understand the courage of the Sidhe who were willing to connect with us humans. It must be exhausting to constantly protect yourself.

HOW HUMANS AFFECT THE SIDHE

The idea of protection raised another question for me. There was the separation in consciousness and vibration as well as what seemed to be a separation in space. Based on what was shared earlier, the Sidhe did not enjoy being in the same space occupied by humans, even though there is a separation in realities. Apparently, these realities were not as separated as the Sidhe would have preferred. Having calmed down my thoughts, I felt that I could reconnect with my friends, and indeed, they responded.

We are grateful that you understand our need to withdraw from you. Most people would take this personally, but we feel only understanding from you. For us, it sparks hope that we can understand each other on a deeper level, find increasing ways to collaborate, and stay connected over longer periods of time.

Let us return to the subject: Rather early in the history of the process of separation, separate worlds were built. Maybe we should say that the Sidhe built a separate world, and the faction that became human went deeper into the physical world. After a long period of time, those who became human went so deep into the material world that they could no longer connect with their origin. They began to forget who they were. They began to see the Sidhe as a different species. As time went on (and due to genetic modifications), humans began to isolate themselves even more from all around them. It was in that phase that humans began to attack us, forcing us to withdraw physically.

The separation was not yet so far along that they could not see us. It was in response to these attacks that the Sidhe worked on creating further separation. The fact that humans began to narrow the vibrational system of their world even more made the separation of the two worlds a necessity; therefore, the Sidhe completed the separation.

As you might be aware by now, the fact that our worlds are separated in frequency does not mean that there is no exchange of energies. For that reason, the Sidhe moved out of the areas where human beings were living. Human emotions became increasingly negative as they penetrated our world. Therefore, we felt we needed a geographic separation. We were fortunate that at a certain moment, almost all humans had forgotten about us, so there were few thoughts, and thus energies, directed toward us.

But the plight for the Sidhe was not over. The human race began to expand, especially in the past couple of hundred years. This expansion has taken on such a form that the human race again threatens the existence of the Sidhe. Many of us are living underground or in remote areas, but we are no longer free from human influence. Humans truly have taken over this planet.

The Sidhe are not the only ones suffering. As a consequence, some of us felt that something needed to be done. There are few ways nowadays to avoid humans. The power of their consciousness is increasing, and now their emotions and thoughts significantly penetrate the energy fields of the Sidhe. The reactions among the Sidhe vary considerably. We represent the faction that believes the only way for us to survive will be to create a new consciousness. We were supposed to be one race, and it seems that circumstances force us to realize that this is still the only way.

There are many among the Sidhe who believe that this is a one-sided solution. The Sidhe are the ones who lose, and the humans gain. We would like to explore this aspect with you and ask a question: Do you believe that the Sidhe are the only ones who lose and sacrifice when the two races move into a world in which we become one?

I was surprised by such a direct question. The pattern with which I am familiar is that the Sidhe connect with humans, tell their story, and offer their suggestions. If we wished to create a new consciousness, equality is mandatory. Some people present the Sidhe as if they have more knowledge and are more advanced than we are. I began to realize that this all depends on your perspective. My feeling is that both Sidhe and humans gain from their interactions and learn from each other how to create a consciousness that is capable of fulfilling their agreement with Gaia.

I conveyed that I believe both races have to sacrifice something in order to create the new consciousness, and that something is safety. For the Sidhe, safety would be defined as living in alignment with a world that you believe represents the Sidhe way. Based on what had been have shared with me, at least some Sidhe are aware that this "safety" has been created by losing the ability to fulfill their agreement with Gaia, that is, helping to raise the vibration of Gaia as a whole to prepare for ascension of the whole system. That means the safety of the Sidhe is a system based on fear and limitation. It has locked up the Sidhe in a morphogenetic grid system that isolates them from many other aspects of Gaia, not only from the human race. The grid has become a prison in which the Sidhe feel comfortable. It may be worthwhile to be free of such a prison.

The human race has also created a prison. This prison is characterized by the word "separation." Like the Sidhe, we created our morphogenetic grid, which now holds us in a prison. It now separates us from most of the world we live in. Most people are not even aware that there is something outside this collective prison. The human prison has many uncomfortable and even horrible aspects. The separation has gone too far.

We create separation within our own species. Some go further than others, depicting those who are different as something that needs to be destroyed. Genocide is still rampant today. What is bizarre is that this is the world humans do not desire to leave. Given that we think that we know how this world works, we create a feeling of safety, even when we feel threatened. Safety is the idea of having a reference to something familiar, and without such a reference, we feel lost. The idea of feeling safe in a known world is similar for both humans and the Sidhe, even though the actual reference systems are notably different.

Both the Sidhe and humans have to sacrifice something. We have to let go of the comfortable, the known, for the unknown territory. We can only undertake this journey if we truly believe. Brave ones must stand up and declare, "Let us explore." Through exploration and sharing, we might be able to create that new world with new reference points for a consciousness that works for both Sidhe and humans.

Personally, I am very happy with the life I have. I am very comfortable with it, and from that perspective, I do not wish to change. However, because I feel the truth that we are missing the fulfillment of our purpose, I am willing to give up something I enjoy for something with which I am unfamiliar. I am acutely aware that change may initially create chaos.

MOVING FROM THE MORPHOGENETIC GRID INTO THE MORPHOGENETIC FIELD

After my sharing, there was no reaction for quite a while. I began to wonder whether I had talked too much or had said something wrong. Then to my surprise, they asked me another question. They referred to my statement that the morphogenetic grids were a kind of prison. They asked me what my opinion was about the morphogenetic field.

I wished they had not asked me that question. During a recent meditation,

I wanted to see how it felt to move out of our current morphogenetic grid and into the morphogenetic field. I could feel myself moving through the frequencies of the grid, and I felt happy. I expected that at any moment I would shoot out of the energies of the morphogenetic grid into the field, but I suddenly hit an energetic barrier. I literally felt it on top of my head: It felt as if I had hit a ceiling.

I was shocked and frustrated. I was not able to escape the grid and move into the field. It seemed that my casual expression — being locked in the grid system — turned out to be a shocking reality. Nevertheless, I still sense that this morphogenetic field is very expansive, holding the full potential of all of our individual and collective abilities as a species. However, having a sense of something is distinctly different from being fully attuned to it.

It might be that considerable preparation is needed for us humans before our systems are ready and able to work with the potential of the morphogenetic field. It could be that a system that is so attuned to limitations would not be able to handle the vast expansion that the morphogenetic field offers. Maybe I should be grateful that I could not move into the field yet. The process might need to be more gradual.

I believe that this full potential of the morphogenetic field is the same for both our races. That brought up a question for the Sidhe: Are they able to escape from the grid and move into the field? My Sidhe friends were apparently pondering over my answer or my question or both, because there was, again, a long pause before they responded.

As you might understand by now, our orientation has never been toward the energies of Earth. We were not aware of what you call a morphogenetic grid. However, the wise among our people understand what you are talking about. The fact that there is no real awareness of the morphogenetic grid almost automatically precludes an awareness of the morphogenetic field.

Your comment that you feel we are locked up in our grid makes sense to at least some of the Sidhe. They define it as being stagnant and not being able to move forward. The Sidhe have created a world separate from humans that has existed for a long time. There has been minimal change, only an intensification of what already exists in our world. In a sense, our world is much more dynamic than yours, but from the perspective of change, your world is much more dynamic than ours.

We will look at what you have shared about the morphogenetic system to understand more fully what this all means for us. We feel, however, that both races might have to look for ways to get out of the confinements of our self-created prisons. We would like to invite you to look at ways that humans can do that as we will look at what we can do. We feel that for now we have explored all that is possible about this subject. We are very grateful for this sharing.

I thanked them as well. I feel the need to look for ways to weaken the walls of these prisons so that we can create a way out. I feel that this could be a major aspect of the mission to create a new consciousness. There simply is no way to create this new consciousness if we stay locked in the prison of our respective morphogenetic grids. Sharing could lead to ways for both races to break down the walls of our individual prisons so that we are free to build the foundation of a new consciousness.

CHAPTER 5

THOUGHTS AND EMOTIONS

M y connections with ShaRaEl and KiRaEl were deepening with every sharing. Their energies became very familiar, and I knew that I had dreams about them even though I could not remember details. They became a part of my thinking in my daily life. It amazed me how quickly they had become a part of my life. I was aware that this was a phase that could end soon, but this was a powerful, intense, and very new experience for me. For the sake of simplicity, they suggested that I use abbreviations of their names and refer to them as Sha and Ki.

THOUGHTS AND EMOTIONS CAN CREATE BARRIERS

During the interactions with Sha and Ki, I felt that their way of interacting with the world was different from mine and from humans in general. I especially felt differences in their way of expressing emotions. It is not easy to describe what I mean. It seemed that their emotions were similar to ours but that there were differences in intensity. It also seemed that their mental abilities had developed far beyond ours. If we decided to work together on a deeper level, it was important to share our emotions and thoughts with each other, which could lead to a deeper understanding of each other.

I believed that a deeper understanding of each other's abilities would lead to a deeper respect for each other, and in turn, this would lead to a more fruitful collaboration. I raised this subject during one of our

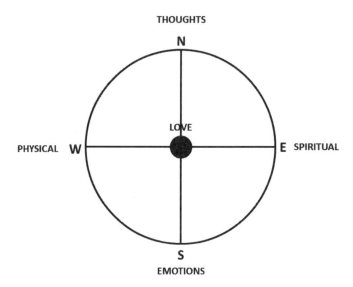

Image 5.1: The four aspects of the human system and love in the center, bringing all in harmony.

interactions. Both Sha and Ki felt that it was indeed important to explore these subjects and to start sharing our ideas and points of view. True to our evolving pattern of interaction, they preferred that I shared first. They asked me to share how humans are dealing with these subjects.

Although there are many ways to explain this subject, I prefer to explain the role and the importance of emotions and thoughts through the use of a symbol: the circle with a cross (see image 5.1). The cross hits the circle at four points, and these points are called the four directions. Each of these four directions can represent many things depending on the subject. Within the context of what we are talking about, the four directions represent the four main aspects of the human system.

In the east, we have the spiritual essence. This is the place where we set an intention, which is the basis of what we wish to create. Opposite from the east is the west. This is the place of physicality and manifestation. It is the place where we see in our world the manifested result based on the intention that we have set in the east. The nature of the result depends to a large degree on the north-south axis, which is defined as the mind. We define the mind as the total summation of all of our emotional experiences and beliefs. The emotions are found in the south. We define emotions as the foundation of creativity. In the north, we have the place of thoughts. These thoughts define the quality and vitality of our creations.

Many people experience the world as challenging because they do not receive what they desire. They believe that they have set a clear intention yet do not experience the results that they were expecting. They are insufficiently aware of the fact that their minds jeopardize their results. They are unaware because they believe that their minds tell them the truth. However, their minds create their thoughts and, in turn, their thoughts induce their emotions. These emotions often prevent the expected manifestation.

The word "emotion" actually describes the importance of emotions very well. Emotion can be described as energy in motion. Emotions need to flow like water, which is the physical expression of the element of water. However, many people do not express their emotions, and consequently, the unexpressed energies are locked within their systems, creating tension. This, then, creates fatigue because so much energy is used to keep these emotions locked inside. Moreover, these locked emotions also create frustration and unhappiness.

Many emotions are based on fear. There is joy, happiness, and love, but for most people, these states are less common than fear, worry, anxiety, frustration, anger, sadness, and other similar emotions that produce unhappiness and eliminate joy.

I surmise that many people spend more time feeling unhappy, stressed, irritated, and frustrated than feeling happy, joyful, and loving because of their emotional states and the consequent thoughts they hold about life. Such emotions and thoughts are powerful barriers to the creation of what is so desired.

PHYSICAL AND SPIRITUAL CREATION

There is another important aspect of the human way of living that I would like to discuss. Most people are insufficiently connected to their spiritual essences, so they create from their thoughts. They also work with their emotional states, often unaware, producing tangible results (see manifestation in image 5.2). This process rarely results in a manifestation of what is desired. These people are unaware of all these emotional aspects and that these emotions play such an important role in their creations. Therefore, people who live this way are usually unhappy and rarely receive what they desire. I call

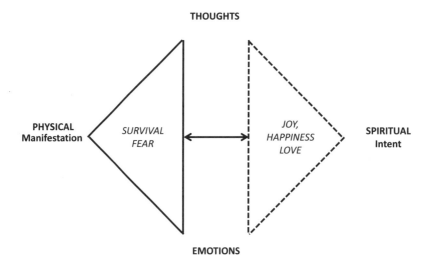

Image 5.2: Displayed are two ways of creating reality: from a physical perspective (left) and a spiritual perspective (right). We need to integrate these two ways.

this ego-driven creation. It is based on personal need, not on love or on the needs of the greater whole.

The right side of image 5.2 shows how our ancestors created before they journeyed more deeply into physical reality. They created from their spiritual essence, which is always connected with the greater good of all through the higher emotions of love, joy, and happiness. Purity of thought draws vitality into creation. Our agreement asked us to merge the physical and the spiritual approaches of creation to produce balance and harmony, thereby evolving us to increasingly higher vibrations. Obviously, this did not work out as originally planned. The physical aspects became dominant in humans, mostly resulting in unhappiness without the means to raise vibrations. Having shared these key elements, I was curious what the Sidhe had to say.

We would like to thank you for your sharing. We always do the best we can to follow and understand what you share. We are getting used to your way of thinking and the way you show us what you are telling us. Your images are very helpful because we also like to work with images. They are easier to understand than words.

It may surprise you to know that we do not analyze the way our systems work as you do. We know how to work with the systems without the need to go through their separate aspects. Therefore, we cannot share with you in the same clarity or with images how our system works. The main reason is that there is a fundamental difference between your system and ours.

You have a considerable delay between thought or intention and manifestation. It is not the same for us. Whatever we think immediately becomes our reality. This can happen so quickly that what we think can immediately change our environment. If we were to take over a thought from you, it would have an immediate and personal effect on us, and it could also affect our world.

We have perfected the ability to change our world immediately. This has many advantages because it allows us to create the world that you call the Sidhe world. That is also the reason that after millions of years, our world is very different from yours. We intended our world to be different by separating it from your world and from humans, who we saw as increasingly threatening and now represent real danger.

This ability to change our world instantly also has disadvantages. There are thoughts that we do not wish to see manifested within our community and our world. Therefore, we have learned to separate, to disconnect from the community when we, for certain reasons, choose to have thoughts that we do not want to affect the whole community. This means that although we are telepathic, we are able to have private thoughts in addition to collective thoughts.

The collective thoughts are the thoughts that we share telepathically with the whole community. Even within the telepathic sharing with our community, we make a separation between two types of thoughts. We separate thoughts that are part of the explorations of our world or that of yours and the sharing that helps us to connect to thoughts that help the community as a whole. It is the last type of thoughts that create our world immediately, and we call this process community building.

Community building could change the whole community. It can change structures and even our environment. Because it is so different from the way your world works, it might be difficult for you to believe. It also makes it difficult to explain, because you do not experience that your world works this way in your reality.

From a very young age, we were trained in these three main ways of thinking. We were trained to be fully aware that every change in us meant or can mean a change in the community. You might now understand that we are very careful in our connections with humans. There is fear among the Sidhe that through our connections with human thoughts and energies, humans might come into our world or community and affect the community in ways that are seen as undesirable. Even though we are separated in many ways, the Sidhe are still receptive and sensitive to human emotions and thoughts.

In our world, we have the freedom to be who we are. Due to our training, we have never encountered a situation that has threatened our society. Whenever there was a threat, it always came from the outside. Therefore, we have never developed a system that forbids us to do what we choose to do. Even when a community would prefer that a Sidhe not do something, we have no means of enforcement. This has created a wonderful unity among the Sidhe that also makes it very difficult for us to see that our community is no longer as homogenous in its thinking as it used to be.

We would like to be clear about the word "homogenous." Because of the freedom we have to express ourselves, there is a large diversity within our society. However, we are homogenous in the overall direction we believe the community needs to go. For the first time in a very long period, that is now changing. There are differences of opinion within the community about the best direction. For the first time, we talk about real change, and that brings up many reactions within our world.

Sha and Ki fell silent. Now that we were getting to know each other better, I could feel that connecting with humans was a difficult and sensitive subject for the Sidhe. It became clearer that such a great change in a society that had been stable internally and mostly unchanging was a big endeavor. To change, they needed to work with the same people from which they had protected themselves for eons and who actually threatened the very foundation of their world.

HOW THE SIDHE DESCRIBE EMOTION

I am aware that the change seemed different for us. The Sidhe were not threatening us. We seemed only to benefit from their willingness to start working with us. However, as was explained earlier, when it came to safety, it was not that simple.

What I noticed in the Sidhe sharing was that they talked about how their thoughts instantaneously created their reality. They did not once use the word "emotions." I was curious whether that was done purposely. When we reconnected, I asked them about it.

Based on what we have observed with humans and on what you showed us in your images, we would say that we do not separate thoughts and emotions. To use your terms, we have developed a "mind" that seems to be mainly "thoughts." Within our thoughts, we feel fluctuations, nuances, that you might call emotions. However, we do not experience emotions in the same way you do.

Based on what we have experienced with you and on what we feel with you, we can only conclude that your emotions have a lot of power. They also contribute certain vividness and a dynamic to your life and your creations that is unfamiliar to us. It seems that when we saw human beings becoming more emotional, we also saw the chaos that emotions created in your world. For that reason, we have chosen to avoid emotions as much as possible. We created a reality in which the mastery of thoughts was extremely important.

In our connection with what you call star nations, we see a similar situation. Many star nations have learned to control emotions because emotions create unpredictable and often unstable states. At the same time, we noticed that many of these star races have a growing tendency to reconnect with emotions. This indicates that emotions are important, and your images have helped us to better understand this. We feel that you have more information to share on this subject that could be helpful to us.

They were right.

EXPERIENCING THE ELEMENTAL FORCES

While the Sidhe were talking, I wondered what they knew about the elemental forces. I have talked about these forces in many of my workshops. Their comment suggested that they might have connected with that information held within my mind. To explain more fully the information about which they were asking, I offered another image based on the same symbol but now using the names of the four elements (see image 5.3).

As I understand it, and as it is shared in the *Sefir Yetzirah*,[1] originally there were only three elements: fire, water, and air. These are called the three mother elements and they were the elements of creation and the basis of the trinity of oneness: the feminine (water), masculine (fire), and child (air). In nonphysical worlds, these elements and associated fundamental principles are enough to create all that is desired. Fire is the conscious intent, which is energy and information. Information is received by the water, by the mother who creates (sets energy into motion, i.e., emotions). The element of air is the breath of the Creator who brings life to the creation: the child.

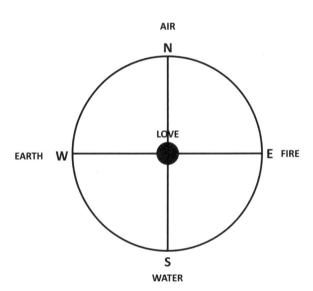

Image 5.3: The four elemental powers.

To create a physical form — a physical manifestation — a fourth element is needed. We call that element earth. The element of earth is not a mother element but comes forth from the three mother elements and thus contains aspects of each. This is creation as the sages of the human race understand it. It indicates the importance of the role of emotions.

However, the human race forgot the understanding of the element of earth, the physical reality. Thus, it can be understood now in image 5.2 that due to the addition of the element of earth, the mental state (thoughts) and the emotions can now be determined by either the needs of the physical or by the essence of the spiritual. We, as a race, became lost in the emotions and thoughts that are connected with survival within the physical reality, and to a large degree, we disconnected from the emotions and thoughts connected with the spiritual essence. I asked my Sidhe friends whether this explanation helped them to understand both the human perspective and the higher perspective of the power of emotions.

As we said earlier, you have the ability to explain processes and systems. As we already mentioned, we do not do this in the same way in our world. Your explanation, however, helps us to explain more about the way we create and stand in life. We would say that we now realize that the Sidhe never connected very deeply with the element of earth.

It might be correct to say that we tried to continue to create in the way that you described creation in the nonphysical world. Even though we live on Earth and are physical, we are far less physical than you are. We are more etheric, as you would call us, closer to what you call the astral world. We can see without difficulty all the human souls who are still bound to Earth, wandering in a state in which they stay connected to their astral bodies. In that sense, we are only partly incarnated in this world. Although we manifest and are part of the physical reality, we manifest in an astral type of world; therefore, we can create instantly.

We are still searching for a description of our emotions. We do have them. For example, you could say that we have fear. We are afraid that we will be unable to maintain the world we live in.

However, this fear is more of a mental fear, an awareness that this can happen. It is not an emotion that influences us in a way that makes us lose ourselves as we see humans do.

Maybe we should use the terminology we heard you use. We see humans as dangerous, and we need to do something about it. Therefore, what we experience may not be fear in the same way as you do, and for that reason it may not be the correct word. [I left this part in the text without editing because it reflects well the search for a meaning of the terms that we use. A sharing does not always flow as smoothly as it seems when you read the text, and this is a nice example of that.]

Your description of the element of water as the element of creation is something we recognize. In that sense, we use emotions. We realize that we have used some of your terms in an incorrect way.

In summary, we would say that it seems that the Sidhe use all four elements in similar ways as you do. The main difference is the vibration of the manifestation. For you humans, it is physically dense and solid, and for us, it is astral-like, pliable, dynamic, and more fluid. We mainly use the energies of the right triangle in your image [image 5.2], but human beings have the tendency to use those of the left triangle more predominantly.

We feel that this sharing has been very beneficial in many ways. It has helped us to better understand what happens in your world with respect to thoughts, emotions, and creation. We hope that you also have a better idea how these aspects work in our world. Although there is quite a gap that needs to be bridged between our two races, we feel that emotions might not be one of the major obstacles. It seems that it will depend mainly on the willingness of human beings to train their minds.

This was a moment when I almost started laughing. I thanked them for their optimism. Training the mind is a major aspect for many people on their spiritual paths. As we humans all know, it is not that easy to master our minds. This is something with which I feel the Sidhe can help us.

The Sidhe are right when they say that it depends on the willingness of human beings to train their minds. For me, there is no doubt that the way to break free from our morphogenetic grid system is by training our minds, because it is through our minds that we are locked in the grid. It may be possible that we can change our thoughts of being limited by beliefs that we are able to control the directions of our lives. We can do this by learning to work from our divine essence. We might be able to break free much faster than we think.

MEDITATION TO HELP RAISE YOUR VIBRATION

I will give a short but powerful meditation that will help you to raise your vibration. It will also help you deepen your connection with the Sidhe. It is a powerful preparation for the ability to connect with the morphogenetic field, which is the most optimal way to escape from the confinements of the morphogenetic grid. The framework of the meditation is similar to the meditation that was given in chapter 3. It also provides the basis for meditations that will be given in forthcoming chapters.

- *Close your eyes, and make yourself as comfortable as possible.*
- *Take a few deep breaths, and begin to relax. Focus on your breathing to relax more deeply.*
- *Just relax; go deeper and deeper.*
- *Bring your awareness to the center of your heart. This is the location of your divine essence. Imagine this essence as a sphere of white light. Allow this white light to radiate out and to shine throughout your physical system. Let it shine into every corner, into every cell.*
- *Feel how this white light holds love that now has spread throughout your physical system. Direct this love to yourself. Feel unconditional love for yourself, exactly as you are now.*
- *Now set the intention that through the connection with your divine essence, you will raise your vibration to the most optimal state possible for you in this moment. Feel your vibration increasing, and trust that it will only go to the most optimal state possible for you in this moment.*
- *Sit in this energy for as long as it feels comfortable for you, and allow the process to unfold.*
- *When you feel ready, take a deep breath. Become aware of your physical body again — feel your feet or butt on the ground or chair — and open your eyes.*

If you are serious about raising your vibration, do this meditation as often as it feels right for you. The frequency of doing this meditation is more important than the duration. Doing this a couple of times each day for a couple of minutes has more effect than, for example, sitting one time for half an hour. This meditation will increase your vibration over time, and it might be the most powerful tool to help us transcend the limitations of the morpho-genetic grid and expand into the morphogenetic field.

CHAPTER 6

ENERGY SYSTEMS AND HEALING

My interactions with the Sidhe had a remarkable impact on me. It is not easy to describe the nature of this impact. Because of our improved communication, my brain was working differently. I also noticed that I perceived things differently, more intuitively and more from an energy perspective than from a physical perspective. It almost felt as if I were a bit Sidhe. It was very subtle yet undeniable.

I also noticed that I was sleeping more deeply and required more sleep. I believe that I processed our interactions during dreamtime. I could hardly wake up, but once I had meditated and completed my exercises, I felt much better. During the rest of the day, I felt well, full of energy and excitement about my interactions with the Sidhe.

At the same time, I noticed that my mind was restless. I pondered the information we had shared. I realized that we were really only at the beginning of understanding each other and still far from actually working together. I noticed that my goals had been adjusted to levels that were more realistic. I had begun to understand the big differences in the way the Sidhe and humans experienced their worlds. Therefore, the first phase was truly to explore each other's worlds to learn about each other while learning more about ourselves. It became clear that we have valuable information to offer each other.

One of the main questions that resulted from our discussions of emotions and thoughts related to the possible differences between the energy systems of the Sidhe and humans. After all, humans are more physically oriented while the Sidhe are more oriented toward an etheric/astral perspective. That in itself is a huge difference. My next question was this: Can we learn from the energy systems of the Sidhe and from the healing modalities they use in their society? Sha and Ki's immediate reactions were most positive.

> Yes, we would love to share with you about our energy systems and how we approach healing. We have already noticed quite some differences between the two races. However, before we start with our sharing, we would highly appreciate a short summary of how you perceive the human energy system. You might wonder why we do it this way.
>
> What we learned in our sharing with you is that the differences in systems — in ways of thinking, in ways of perceiving — are quite considerable. By listening to your summary, we learn from your mind what you mean by certain terms and descriptions, and it makes it easier to explain our part in a way that is more understandable for you. In that way, we both learn from each other, and it brings us closer together.

THE HUMAN ENERGY SYSTEM

When the Sidhe asked me to provide an introduction of the subject, it made me aware that asking a question is easy, but answering it often is not. Books have been written about the different aspects of our energy systems, and I also have no doubt that books can be filled with information about the Sidhe energy systems (although I doubt they have books). Here we condensed everything about energy systems and healing into one chapter. The Sidhe tell me that this is sufficient for this phase.

We are connecting and sharing within a limited framework of communication, exploring each other's way of thinking, experiencing, and living. It is an orientation, and time will tell whether we can go deeper into certain subjects and what these subjects need to be to create a new consciousness. So I took a deep breath and presented the following summary of the human system.

Most people in our world are mainly focused on their physical bodies.

Whenever there is pain or dysfunction, they go to see a doctor. The doctor either prescribes a chemical compound to heal the ailment or sends the patient to a specialist. Although I am aware that I am generalizing, the main point I want to make is that the traditional modern medicine still used by the majority of humankind is based on analyzing parts instead of the whole. There is an increase in the development of holistic healing based on the human system as a whole, and different energy modalities are used. However, we have developed many modalities and are still developing new ones because we have the idea that the human system is complex. Therefore, we need many different systems for healing.

The truth, however, is that we are not truly holistic because we still do not fully understand the human system as a whole in all its aspects. Most people who learn an energy method for healing apply this method without really knowing what they are doing. I am not saying this to be critical but purely from my perception of our approach to understanding and healing the human system.

Because we are so physically oriented, there are many people who look specifically at food. There are endless opinions to process; thus, people either give up, not knowing the truth about this subject, or they decide to follow a particular system. In other words, humans do not have the ability to know through a deeper connection within themselves what they need and what they do not need. We have lost this ability; therefore, we need a system that somebody designs for us. Although there are early signs of change, there is still a long way to go.

In addition to the physical system, we are aware of and are able to describe three main systems: the meridian system, the chakra system, and the aura (or energy field around the human body). The meridian system, as it is used, is generally based on traditional Chinese medicine. Working with the meridian system has been well integrated in the Western world. It can be described as a system of channels through which life force flows. The main flows are connected with different organs in the body. There are fourteen major meridian flows.

There are specific energy points within the meridians that are called acupuncture points. These are the points through which a practitioner helps to regulate the flow through the meridians. They either diminish the flow (if there is too much energy) or stimulate it (if there is not enough energy). Although this description is very simplified, it reflects the basic principle. Generally, there are 361 points that are used for acupuncture treatments. There are other modalities that work with meridian flows, and they also use energy points on the meridians, although the points can differ from those used in acupuncture. Two of these modalities are Shiatsu (or acupressure) and Jin Shin Jytsu. The meridians operate within the physical, etheric, and astral bodies of the human system.[1]

Most alternative and energy healers view the chakras as the most important energy system. For them, it is the easiest energy system to work with. Chakras are energy centers with a spiraling energy that connects the physical body with the energy bodies of a human being as well as with the outside world. Most resources available will define seven chakras in the human body. Based on recent research I have done, I have defined twelve chakras connected with the human physical system.[2] Actually, there are fourteen chakras, of which three chakras form a heart chakra complex. Therefore, these three heart chakras can be seen as one system, hence the number twelve.[3]

I see chakras as fractal energy of the white light of the soul. This fractioning happens when the white light of the soul enters into the physical system. Because of the way humans function, our chakras are no longer in optimal states, and the soul is unable to express itself properly through the physical system. There is awareness that it is very important to transform and heal all of the issues that prevent the chakras from working optimally so as to be able to allow the soul to fulfill its purpose. Although all those who work with the chakras might not express this similarly, most modalities that involve the chakras have a similar focus.

An important aspect is the flow of energies through the chakras. There are three main channels, called *nadis*, that flow through the chakras. These nadis, that flow through seven or twelve chakras or through both the seven and twelve chakras at the same time.[4] It may sound complicated, but it is simple once you understand it. The essence of the chakras is to make sure that the energy through the nadis can flow uninterrupted, once again allowing the light of the soul to shine and to become, as we call it, enlightened.

The last part of the human energy system is the aura. The aura is composed of five main energy bodies,[5] but some people believe that there are many more. There are also many energy layers (more than a hundred), and these layers are part of the five energy bodies. The energy bodies reflect the condition of the physical body and the way we function in this world.

THE SIDHE ENERGY SYSTEM

I was aware that I had given a generalized, and perhaps rather superficial, summary of the human energy system. I had no clue whether this was enough for the Sidhe to work with and to gain a reasonable understanding of it. Of course, I was also very curious about what they had to say. By this time, I was used to the silence after my sharing, knowing that their response would come.

We understand that you call your summary short. With such an expansive subject, it is good in the first instance not to go into too many details. In this phase, it is not clear which details are important for the journey that we have embarked on together. This journey is not about working out all the details about each other's systems, ways of living, and perceptions. That could take lifetimes given the many differences and given the fact that especially humans barely understand their own energy systems.

The journey is about sharing those aspects of the different subjects that will enable us to connect more deeply with each other and to see what aspects are helpful for further collaboration and for developing a new consciousness that will help to bridge the consciousness of the Sidhe with the humans'.

We read a reaction in your mind, and you are right. It is not so much to bridge the consciousness of our two races but more a way to find access to the morphogenetic field that will make it possible to break free from the restrictions of the boxed-in consciousness of the grids that both races are locked into. This access is, of course, for those who choose to free themselves. We are both aware that this might not be motivating for all humans and Sidhe.

We will also try not to give a detailed description of our systems but share what seems relevant for this phase. Thanks to your sharing, we will be able to give you at least an impression of the differences and the similarities. To begin with, as you know by now, we are not as physical as you are. Consequently, we also approach our systems not so much from a physical perspective.

All that you describe as organs and other bodily parts, we also have, but they are more etheric/astral. From your point of view, this means they are not physical at all. You call them energetic imprints, but we call them physical. There are many similarities to our systems. That is why we can make ourselves visible to some of you, and what you will see is basically a human-like being.

From your perspective, we are more energy than physical. That means that by definition, there are differences in the way the energy systems function. The most striking difference would be for you to learn that we do not have chakras or meridian points. This is a consequence of the fact that we do not have physical bodies that reflect the physical system of Earth. By going more deeply into physical matter, you reflect the energy systems of Earth more strongly, just as all physical beings on Earth do to various degrees. We have tried everything to make sure that we would not sink into physicality so that the same would not happen to us.

This does not mean that we do not have energy systems. We need them as much as you do. The best way to make a comparison between our systems is by saying that we have energy flows that have similarities with your meridians and nadis. In your description, you did not share what factors influence these energy flows in a way that an imbalance is created and rebalancing is needed. Can you share a bit more about that?

THE DIFFERENCES OF THE MIND

I realized that I might not have been very clear about that, so I explain further. From the moment that we are born, we receive messages and energies from our environment. This is mainly from our parents, but depending on the society, others may be involved as well, such as family members and people who are friends or visitors.

Human beings are by definition out of balance in basically every way with very few exceptions. So a child receives messages that create confusion and unbalance. These experiences create emotional conditions and belief structures that define the way the mind begins to work. Most of these emotions and beliefs are survival systems that cause energy systems to go out of balance. The belief structures continue to induce similar experiences that lead to deeper engraining of behavioral patterns, which builds stress that in turn disrupts the flows in the energy systems.

We already talked about the mind. Through their experiences, human beings create minds that keep repeating patterns, beliefs, and emotions. In that way, the mind holds the imbalance of the different energy systems in place, and as time passes, that imbalance becomes even worse.

This helps us to understand the human system better and makes it easier to explain our system. We begin to understand that what you call "mind," we call "thought." We talked about that before. We do not experience emotions as strongly and definitely not in the same way as humans. For the sake of clarity, we will use the term "mind." That makes it easier for you to understand us when we say that our minds influence the way the energies in our energy systems flow.

Based on what you share, we should use your word "nadis" for our energy flows rather than meridians. We feel that the term "nadis" has an energetic value that comes closer to our experience of the flows in our system.

Our nadis can also be out of balance due to our thoughts, our minds. Because of the way we function, the energy flows go out of balance instantly. When we have a misaligned thought, one or more of our nadis will immediately reflect that. It seems that in your society, nobody will notice it when a thought induces unbalance in your system because your systems are more or less off balance permanently.

However, in our society, the Sidhe will notice immediately when somebody's energy flows are out of balance. In addition, the telepathic communications we have will also give a signal when somebody's system is off balance. That is the big difference between our two worlds. You can be out of balance and it goes completely unnoticed, but that is not possible in our society.

The inability to notice when somebody is off balance contributes to an increase in dysfunction in your society. Because you have become so insensitive, you rarely notice it when people need help unless they ask for it or when their behavior becomes so noticeable in its disturbing effects that it can be denied no longer.

From listening to your sharing, it is becoming clearer to us that there is insufficient knowledge about the human system as a whole and insufficient experience and training to help each other to heal. We are aware of your personal healing work, and within your society, you might be successful. Forgive us for what we are about to say, but from our perspective, the healing work you do is quite primitive. It lacks the in-depth knowledge and understanding of energy flows.

We are aware that the physical system complicates things a lot, but it is still the mind that affects the flow in the nadis of your systems. When there is a problem in the flow of our nadis in our systems, we will know what type of thought has induced this problem. We know this by looking at the type of nadi that has been influenced. We do not work with every small energy flow. We have defined the nadis that are directly affected by thoughts and are the ones that might go out of alignment first. We are aware that the flows in our system are not the same as in your system. Again, there are many similarities, but the systems are not identical. Therefore, we cannot define the relationship between thoughts and specific nadis in your system because we are not used to the powerful effect that the physical body has on all your energy systems. In addition, we do not understand the minds of human beings. We would call your minds erratic and completely illogical.

SIDHE HEALING

This was a moment for me to jump in. My ego was unhappy to hear that my healing methods were primitive, but I could not deny that even with all of my study and training, I have more questions than answers. I am very aware that we lack insight and knowledge with respect to the workings of our energy systems. I agree that our modalities are rather primitive, but I would prefer the expression "in an early stage."

A more important point is that we have some degree of understanding of the relationship between certain energy flows and certain emotions and

emotional thoughts. Traditional Chinese medicine has taught us the relationship between meridians and emotions.[5] I am sure that there is much more to
understand, but it is an important beginning.

Finally, the fact that we have meridian points and chakras as part of our
energy system make our two systems less comparable than the Sidhe suggest.
Through these points and chakras, there is a strong interaction with the outside world that, as far as I understand, does not exist to the same degree in
the Sidhe world.

I was not sure how my Sidhe friends would react to my feedback. However, I felt a lot of love coming from them, which made me feel really happy.

We are grateful for your reply. This sharing is truly helpful in understanding each other's world. Thanks to your reaction, we can now
see clearly what we could not see before. You also reminded us that
your world is very challenging for you and even threatening for us.
We cannot begin to imagine what it means to live in your world and
maintain a high level of vibration. We thank you for this reminder. In
creating an energy bubble in which we can communicate safely, we
forget the type of energies that are present in your world.

To return to the nadis and meridians, we now better understand
the difference between us. We would like to share one more aspect
of our energy systems. You shared several aspects of healing, and we
wish to share a few things about our healing.

Our education is quite different from yours. We would like to
spend more time looking at education in a future sharing. Part of our
education is to learn to become aware of our energy flows and overall
energy condition. We are also trained to be aware of that in others.
Based on what we have been told, this was the key to the survival of
our race. We could not allow the existence of any disturbing energies
that might lower our vibrations, because that could bring us deeper
into the physical system and closer to what we have always tried to
avoid: becoming more like humans.

Therefore, we have built energy awareness into our way of living
to a degree that you might call obsessive. This is deeply built into
everything we do. Any lowering of vibration in any person is noticed

and measures are taken, either by the person or by the community, to bring the system back into balance. It is this ability to maintain a very high standard of permanent high frequency in every aspect of our society that begins to fail. The energetic effect of the ever-expanding human race on our world is increasing, and there are clear signs that it becomes difficult for our society to maintain that high state of vibration.

There are an increasing number of beings in our race who need help to maintain their energy balance. The group that interacts with human beings sees this as a sign that the Sidhe are no longer able to maintain complete separation of our worlds. The Sidhe always withdraw themselves from all that may be a threat to their energy system. We are now at a point that this becomes increasingly difficult, and soon it might be impossible.

The group that interacts with humans believes that Gaia holds a system of interconnecting beings and energies so that you can never really be separated from each other, which both humans and Sidhe are experiencing. Separation is a consciousness aspect, not a reality. Separation exists as long as you believe that it exists. Separation is an illusion that induces tension because it negates the fact that Gaia is one dynamic, interactive system. This realization might help us to create a new way of being on Earth, and through creating a new consciousness, we might be able to fulfill the purpose and agreement that our common ancestors were never able to fulfill.

That felt like a wonderful closing of our sharing about energies and healing. As much as the Sidhe seemed to be doing better than human beings, they also needed much healing. After all, healing means "becoming whole," and neither race is whole. Maybe together we can help each other to create the wholeness within each race that will lead to a new consciousness. Then we might be able to do what none of our ancestors were able to do: help the Gaia system to rise in vibration and, ultimately, ascend.

CHAPTER 7

PROCREATION AND HEREDITARY FACTORS

Two subjects that had been mentioned frequently in my previous interactions with the Sidhe raised questions for me. One was the idea that we seemed to have common ancestry. The other was the process that described the separation: that we have grown in different directions over time, creating different races.

The Sidhe had also referred to differences within their race. That raised the question of how different the Sidhe really were from us. This point became even more important when we looked at the morphogenetic systems. It was clear that the morphogenetic grids of the Sidhe and those of humans hold different energies and information. We had already connected with many of these differences, which might be even larger than we thought. At the same time, it seemed that we shared the same morphogenetic field that implied that the differences between our two races had to be held within the space of the morphogenetic field.

In our system, DNA plays an important role in maintaining the characteristics of a species. DNA is also the system through which we pass on our characteristics to our offspring. I became curious about how the Sidhe viewed DNA and how in their less physical systems the Sidhe's characteristics are passed on.

I was also curious about variation within the Sidhe race. We have many sub-races that can intermarry easily and create children. I supposed the same was true for the Sidhe. Finally, I understood that the Sidhe could grow very old, which reminded me of the belief that humans used to live much longer, as is shared in the Bible, for example. Some of the old fathers mentioned in the Old Testament lived up to 900 years.[1] Therefore, I was curious about the thoughts and experiences of the Sidhe with respect to DNA and hereditary traits.

HUMAN DNA STRUCTURE

As a way to induce the proper exchange of information, Sha and Ki asked me to summarize the main aspects of what I knew about hereditary traits and the duration of life for humans.

Humans believe that they know a lot about DNA and the role of the different genes. We have mapped the human genome, the part that we believe forms proteins, which are the building blocks of life. Only part of the total DNA is considered functional. The majority of the DNA is called junk DNA. This junk DNA is mainly seen as remnants from past characteristics, pieces of DNA that we no longer need. The ideas about junk DNA are changing. An increasing number of our scientists now realize that a lot of the junk DNA has regulatory functions, which make it possible to express the many different traits and the complexity that humans possess while at the same time possessing not many more genes than primitive species with fewer characteristics.

While we are still unraveling the function of the different pieces of our DNA, we have discovered another important aspect of the DNA system. There are factors regulating when and where a certain gene expresses itself. All cells have the same information, but they do not have the same function. Therefore, DNA needs to know at each given place within our bodies which aspects need to be expressed and which do not. The system that provides that information can be compared to a software program.

We call the software program that regulates how DNA works at the different places in the body epigenetics. This software program creates tags that tell a gene not to express at certain locations. One of the major tags is the methyl group.

There is another system, the histones, which also functions as software for DNA. They regulate the degree or speed of expression. Methyl groups are on/off switches, and histones are like a regulatory knob. So every cell has a distinct methyl and histone pattern that determines its function in the whole. The methyl group and the histones are the epigenetic factors.

A genome will remain the same during our whole lives. However, epigenetic factors change. They change because functions change during our lives. Such periods are, for example, puberty, pregnancy, and menopause. However, epigenetic factors also might change as a consequence of more subtle changes in our environment, such as the types of food we eat, whether we smoke or use drugs, and our emotional states.

Many of the epigenetic factors are hereditary and consequently can be passed on through a couple of generations. This means that what you do to yourself can have an effect on your children and grandchildren and even great-grandchildren. That is why there are currently many diseases and dysfunctions that are rooted in previous generations, such as obesity, diabetes, cancer, and many others. Once I heard somebody speculate that cancer is the consequence of a misplaced epigenetic tag — the tag being a methyl group.

Because the epigenetic factors are software programs, we can change them. The most important epigenetic factor is fear. When we become fearless, we change epigenetic factors. In addition, when we are fearless, our brains work better, and we can more easily induce changes to the epigenetic factors.

We know that stress is an important factor in determining the length of our lives. There is also the belief that we have a longevity gene that our scientists have been searching for. However, the genes they have currently found might extend our average life expectancy by only a couple of decades.[2] If we truly have a longevity gene, we may all have epigenetic factors that prevent the expression of this gene.

SIDHE DNA STRUCTURE

There is one last thing on this subject that I would like to share. It is a personal belief that is shared only by a few people. It seems to me that the DNA of the human species is totally programmed to function as an antenna for the information in the morphogenetic grid but not for the information located in the morphogenetic field. Assuming that the Sidhe also have DNA, there must be a similar situation for them. They also seem to be attuned to their morphogenetic grid while they are not attuned to the morphogenetic field. I wondered what the Sidhe had to say.

Your sharing always helps us in many ways. We hear your terminology, we feel your thoughts while you share, and we get a better understanding of the human race and where it is on its journey. Your sharing always gives us hope.

We are beginning to see that the Sidhe see the human race as too negative, and we are learning that there are humans with whom we truly can have an exchange that is helpful for the creation of a different consciousness. We are especially interested in all that you share about the difference between the morphogenetic grids and field. Our people are looking at that now as much as we can. But let us go back to the subject of DNA.

Let us start with a statement: We do not have DNA in the form of a chemical structure as you have. However, we do have an energetic structure that basically has the same function. As far as we can feel into your system, you also have such a structure, and some people call that the etheric DNA. Your etheric DNA may have a different kind of antenna function, but it seems to be directly linked to your physical DNA. At this stage, we do not know with certainty whether the etheric DNA is adding information to your system or acting as a precursor for the chemical structure. It seems that it is basically a precursor, but it might be possible that this will change when your vibration changes.

We see our etheric DNA structure (to keep your terminology) as the information system that determines who we are, very similar to what you do with the chemical DNA structure. We never analyzed the different parts; therefore, we have never "mapped" what the different parts are doing. We are aware that the etheric DNA has more information than we use, but in the Sidhe philosophy, that means that we do not need it.

Within our understanding, we do not have what you call epigenetic factors. If we have them, they are most likely very stable. Because we have a powerful system that keeps our energy systems stable, there are not many changes for the sake of our race. Changes were made in the past as a way to protect ourselves.

We also believe in the power of, what you call, the mind. In our history, we are aware of certain changes that we made collectively in order to strengthen certain qualities. We learned in that manner and are now programmed to change our world based on what we desire collectively.

The fact that our systems have such a high stability indicates that we have to be connected with a system that supports that stability. As we understand from you, this is the morphogenetic grid that holds the collective thoughts, information, and programs of our race. As I mentioned before, there is no indication that the Sidhe as a race want change. They only want protection from the influence of humans.

We are an entrenched race, and we see humans as too dynamic with too many — mainly erratic — changes. In our world, we want to stay connected with the morphogenetic information system that supports stability.

I understood the challenge faced by the Sidhe. To remain in Gaia's world as a race that prefers not to change must be extremely difficult. They must possess great power to make that possible. From my perspective, it is a waste of quality and energy. The main characteristic of the world we live in is change, but the Sidhe have created a bubble within that system that is geared toward preventing it. I am glad I am human. I believe that change is the only way to reach my true essence. I am passionate about changing, and I know many share this passion, even though these people form a minority in our society.

We are not only beginning to understand your passion for change but are also beginning to believe that change is important. As difficult as it is for the Sidhe, there is an increasing realization that change might be our only hope and may be our only true protection. We are looking for a way to change in order to survive without losing the essence of being Sidhe.

I found the last comment an interesting one. In previous exchanges, it had become clear that the Sidhe connected with star systems. So I asked a new question: Does that mean the Sidhe also connect with the stars to maintain their stability?

That is correct. We feel that the energies of the different star systems help us to stabilize our energies in order to deal with the energies that come from the physical world of the humans. However, in these connections, we are quite specific with which star systems we want to connect. We select the systems that we believe will strengthen us in being who we are. We do not connect with star systems with which we do not resonate because they might do what humans do to us: bring us out of balance or induce change.

SIDHE PROCREATION

I explained that in the way humans procreate, the mother's DNA from the egg cell combines with the father's DNA from the sperm cell, creating a child that has a mixture of characteristics of both parents. Because Sidhe are not physical, I wondered how that works for them. I felt that this question made the Sidhe uncomfortable. I wondered why. They read my thoughts and responded.

It is a subject that we do not talk about so openly. Because we are not physical, intimacy is more a blending of energies. In a sense, this is also true for humans, but for us, it is a very conscious experience. Procreation is less important for us because we live long lives. However, when we have children, we take the process of guiding children in their lives very seriously. For us, it is unthinkable to do what we see many parents in the human world do.

We see humans create children and then, from our perspective, neglect their education. For us, parenting is a serious issue, given that a child needs to learn to be a member of the society that needs stability. Therefore, the choice for a child is more a community decision than it is an individual decision.

We prefer not to share too much in this phase of our interaction. The choice to have a child and the process of creation is also something in which the community is involved. For us, it is a sacred process. The only thing that we would like to share is that the etheric DNA does not entirely come from the two parents although they are the primary contributors. There are contributions from other members to the degree that is most desirable for the community as a whole. Again, this is a sacred process, and this is not the right time to share much about it.

I then asked whether the Sidhe know the secret of their longevity. The question obviously amused them.

> We do not know, and we never wonder. This is natural for us, and we accept it as part of the life of a Sidhe. We can understand why it is a question for humans, because your lives are so short. We know that in the past, humans had lives of a similar duration to ours, but we believe that the shortening of your lives is a consequence of your descent into physicality. We also believe that the only true way to lengthen your life is to get out of physicality.

What an interesting statement! I never thought about the possibility that our lives became shorter because we became denser. However, our agreement is to raise the vibration of consciousness while being in the physical so that we will be able to raise the vibration of Gaia. Raising our vibration might also be the way to lengthen our lives. As much as it would be nice to have a longer, healthy life, my personal goal is to help create — with (preferably) or without the Sidhe — this new consciousness that will help Gaia as a whole. It may also help both races on their evolutionary paths.

CONNECTIONS WITH THE SIDHE

For me, there were two questions remaining that related to creating a new consciousness. The first one had to do with variation within the Sidhe race. In our initial contact, they referred to differences among the Sidhe. I asked whether any of these differences relate to a difference in genetic makeup.

> Yes, there are some differences. These differences have to do with the fact that different communities make slightly different choices during the sacred ritual of creating a new Sidhe being. However, these differences are not large. They are definitely not so large that it will have an effect on the stability of the race as a whole. Because there are

telepathic connections between the communities, we help each other to make sure that the stability will be maintained.

Initially, I thought about the Sidhe world and their stability as a rather boring one. However, when they talked about the creation of a new Sidhe and how that involves the community, I could feel the deep connection, love, and respect held for each other through this sacred process. It feels so different from how we create children. I am aware that this also can happen in human love, but often passion, sexual desire, lust, or other factors are the driving forces.

Procreation in humans is also determined by religion and social and cultural factors. For example, in many societies, having many children is the only way to make sure that you will be taken care of when you are old. Procreation is definitely something personal that we separate from the community. We truly are quite different.

My last question had to do with the Sidhe who connect with humans. I queried the following: I understand that there is a small group of Sidhe who wish to connect with humans. In what way are they different from the majority of the Sidhe who do not desire change? Is it not contrary to the nature of the Sidhe to desire change?

We love your direct questions. They reflect a genuine longing to get to know us in order to increase the possibility of collaboration. In a sense, you are right. It is almost against the nature of a Sidhe to want to connect with human beings. We do not want to call humans our enemies, but to most Sidhe, you are at least a threat to the survival of our race.

As we said before, most of our race is against a deeper connection with humans. Our race believes, however, that it is better to allow us to have the connection with representatives of your race than to engage in a disagreement among ourselves that will influence the consciousness and stability of the whole. However, the community and even the whole race do observe these interactions closely.

We have had connections with human beings that existed over long periods. In certain areas, these connections occurred more frequently than in others. These connections were almost always incidental, such as the Sidhe helping humans or staying in contact to know what is going on in the human world. In the period that you call the Dark Ages, the Sidhe helped people who had close contact with nature and were persecuted for having this connection. At the same time, this was a period in which many Sidhe felt the necessity to separate themselves even more from human energies and human consciousness.

We share this to help you understand that connections with humans are not uncommon. What is currently different is the attempt to actually communicate. In many societies, the Sidhe who attempt to communicate are called observers. Observers are Sidhe whose task it is to observe what is going on in the human world. The information that they collect helps the Sidhe as a whole to protect themselves, helps communities to decide to move, and helps them to know how to start preparing for the future.

These observers are trained to protect themselves from most of the influence of human energies. However, they can do that only for certain periods. Then they need to recharge in the Sidhe communities. The observers began to notice that there were changes within the human world. There are people who are, what you call, on their spiritual paths, and they began to learn to reconnect with the world and the beings, both visible and subtle, around them. These people were approached by the observers to see whether communication was possible. As you have noticed, the establishment of proper communication is not an easy process. We feel that we are actually doing very well.

I fully agreed with them. We were doing very well. I had come to an understanding that the two Sidhe that I had contact with differed from other Sidhe only in their willingness to connect with humans. Because they observed us, humans were less foreign to them. I expressed my gratitude for their courage to connect and to communicate with me. With that, I could feel we reached a natural ending of this interaction.

I sat awhile longer in amazement that this was happening to me. I never planned to connect with the Sidhe. I remember that John Matthews and David Spangler communicated something similar. It felt that it was happening to me because of all the work I had done previously. The same seemed to be true for David Spangler, John Matthews, and others.

The most amazing aspect of the communication with Sha and Ki was the clarity of the connection. Sometimes it took awhile before we could start, but once we started, the interaction flowed naturally, as if I had done this work my whole life. I had said several times during our interactions, "I wonder where this will lead me." I know that this is an irrelevant question; nonetheless, it keeps coming up. At the same time, I trusted that unfoldment would eventually reveal everything.

CHAPTER 8

TEACHING AND LEARNING: THE EDUCATION SYSTEMS

I n chapter 7, the importance of the education systems of both the Sidhe and humans was mentioned. An education system reflects the way we are taught to look at and perceive the world in which we live. Sha and Ki asked me to give my perspective of the education system that we have in our world.

When children are born in our world, they learn from the people around them and later from the different education systems. Our education systems determine to a large degree how we see the world, what we believe about the world, the way things work in the world, and what motivates or demotivates us. What we experience in the world with all its problems, differences, and fears for others and ourselves — even hate for others — all result from the way we perceive our world. Our experiences determine our emotions, thoughts, actions, passions, and basically everything within us. The major influence on our perception of the world is our education system. I will summarize information that is relevant to explain the way most people see the world in which they live.

HUMAN SCHOOLING

I will restrict this discussion to the education systems that we call schools. Those systems of teaching and learning have an underlying similarity that currently is fairly consistent across the world. Our schools teach us how to function in a materialistic society. We learn how we believe this physical world works and how to become specialized so that we can obtain a trade or job or career to acquire income that provides the comforts that we all desire.

The education system is mainly focused on telling the students how things are ("facts") according to our current beliefs. In our school systems, we need to learn to repeat what we are taught to show that our adaptability is sufficient to become a good member of human society. Everything is geared toward the idea that every child needs to learn a certain basic minimum to become that good member. There are possibilities of individual expression in certain school systems. However, for the most part, there are standards that are determined by government institutions that define what every child needs to master in order to be a "normal" and, above all, "functional" member of society.

Abundant tests are given to check whether the knowledge of a child meets the required standards. If these standards are not met, the child is considered to have problems and to need support to ensure that he or she can adapt within the system as much as possible.

What is taught in schools is often not the most recent knowledge. Because government institutions dictate the main subjects that must be included in a school program, many subjects trail behind current knowledge and wisdom, sometimes by many years. Of course, there are teachers who do their best to add interesting subjects. However, they are limited in their options because of the considerable time that is needed to cover the required curriculum.

Children learn early on in their education program to focus on specific subjects based on personal skills. After we have fed the children with what is called basic information, we train them to become specialists in certain subjects. Therefore, humans are not taught to oversee the whole. This process creates a view that the world is separated into parts, which contributes to living in a world of separation. The idea of separation is increased because all teaching comes from the idea that humans are the most developed and leading species on this planet who have the right to take from Earth all that we believe we need and even whatever we desire. Rarely are children taught to respect other life forms in such a way that they understand we are all connected as one.

Although there are signs of change, most schools work toward educating children to conform to the standards that are set by the system. Children who are not successful in learning the prescribed material have a hard time in most schools. Many children are traumatized in school because they are not able to follow the instructions and then are labeled as unintelligent or as having problems. The schools or connected institutions are often unable to fully support them.

In recent times, an increasing number of children are considered different. They have difficulty with the school system and are diagnosed, for example, with attention deficit disorder (ADD), attention deficit hyperactivity disorder (ADHD), or any number of conditions on the autism spectrum. The major objective (with exceptions) is to do everything to "fit" these children into the system, yet the system adjusts minimally to these increasing numbers of different children. It is deemed so important that the children fit into the system that the use of drugs (such as Ritalin) to ensure that this goal is achieved is unfortunately increasing considerably.

I am aware that although my attitude toward our education system is harsh and probably judgmental, there is truth in my view. In the discussions and vision for creating a new consciousness, I see our current education system to be a formidable obstacle to creating the desired changes. Everything we teach is geared exclusively toward the physical world. With rare exceptions, there are no true spiritual teachings in our schools. The existence of subtle worlds is fundamentally unacceptable in the school curriculum. Children are minimally trained (if at all) to respect and love Earth and all that lives on her. In my opinion, the education system is one-sided. It is oriented toward imprisoning our society within the paradigms that are dictated by governments, religious organizations, and major corporations.

I would like to be clear that I am not criticizing our teachers. Having been a teacher myself, I have learned to respect those who give most of their lives to teach children what they believe they need to learn. They do the best they can within the possibilities that are defined within the school system. My criticism is directed to those who define the school system from a mental idea about how education supports our economic system instead of looking at how the education system should support the creation of loving beings, teaching them to recognize and develop their unique qualities.

I believe people who have a connection with their abilities and have learned to express their qualities optimally are the best support for a healthy society. However, there is no support for the development of the uniqueness of people, unless it is an ability that can be used to support corporations and governments. In a sense, the systems prefer us to be like cattle or sheep so that we can be driven in the direction that the leaders tell us to go. The saddest aspect is that the majority of people are not even aware of all of this. They believe that this is how the system needs to be. If they were aware, they would surely feel at a loss as to how to change it or even how to not be affected by it.

Based on what I have shared, it might be clear that I am considered a rebel who does not support the system that we have created. Fortunately, many people are beginning to look for ways to reconnect with who they truly are after deviating from traditional education institutions.

So far, I have mainly talked about the primary and high school systems. It might seem that colleges and universities are different. However, that is only partially true. In order to receive money for research and education, institutions have to adjust to the requirements of governments and large companies who contribute to the financing of these institutions.

One last aspect must be mentioned now: There are an increasing number of organizations, education institutions, and people who offer independent training and education more directly focused on personal development. However, they have to deal first with deprogramming the existing belief structures before new concepts can be accepted, integrated, and lived. Teachings in these independent organizations might make a difference in the way people see our world. These are still in the early stages of development, but progress is rapid.

One obstacle to progress in their development is insufficient collaboration among institutions. There are many personal visions that color the teachings, but here we are also beginning to see change and attempts to collaborate. Without true collaboration, respect, and support for each other, these alternative teaching systems are no more than variations of a theme that is already abundantly present in our society.

I might have started with a lot of criticism. Nonetheless, I am an optimist. I believe that the human species will change, and I can see many signs of progress. It would be empowering if the official institutions would make it easier for us to find our true essence so that we no longer have to clear so much of what we have been taught to believe about ourselves.

After my sharing, I was ready for some views from my Sidhe friends.

SIDHE SCHOOLING

We feel your pain and frustration as a consequence of the way you perceive your education system. We now know you well enough to understand that you are talking about your experiences when working with people whose issues reflect the results of your education systems both at home and in school. It also helps us to better understand the energies that we perceive from people. As you know, we are afraid of the effect these energies have on us. Therefore, there is a tendency to judge human beings.

Listening to you, we feel this judgment begins to fall away because we are getting a better understanding of the challenges that you are facing. We also better understand your description of being locked up in the box of your morphogenetic grid system. Much will stay in place due to the education system. As we now understand it, education is the most powerful aspect that keeps you in the system of the collective.

Your sharing set something into motion in us as well. You describe your system as rather rigid, and there is a need to free yourself from it. You have a clear motivation to step out of your system to find new ways to discover who you really are. We realize that our system has rigid aspects as well.

While we hear you talk about freeing yourself from the limitations of your education system in the broadest sense of the word, we believe that our education is based on how we believe we need to be, and we believe this is what we really want. Therefore, we do not have the same incentive to see how to get out of our system. You are aware to some degree that you are more than your education system — at least some of you are — and we understand that the number of people who hold that belief is increasing. We think that our education system is who we are and that it totally supports us in being Sidhe. That is the reason that we have hardly changed over eons and why it is challenging to change now.

We do not know the full history of the human race. We are happy about that because your history is characterized by a lot of violence. However, there have also been good periods in your history, and there were phases in which there was such a high level of civilization that we interacted with humans in these periods more than your history is telling you. It seems that your dynamic history keeps humans in a perpetual state of searching for change and new developments. The dynamic history we see with human beings is absent in the history of the Sidhe. The Sidhe always search for stability and for protection against change.

Let us share something about our education. Similar to your world, our education starts after birth. While this aspect of education in your world has become restricted mainly to the parents (and sometimes just one parent), in our world, it is the responsibility of the whole community into which a child is born. We are aware that this approach used to be common among certain cultures in your world, and to some degree, it still is. We are also aware that even though there is telepathic communication among us, a child needs certain individuals for certain aspects of development. There is also the freedom for children to go to those whom they feel attracted to.

Our education is not in a school system as yours is. We also do not have as many children, mainly because we live so long. Small groups of children go to certain individuals for training in how to become supportive members of our world. In that sense, it is not different from your world. The difference, however, is that we adjust completely to the child's individual method or learning. While the way we educate is freer, the goal is still to make sure that a child fits within society.

We are not aware of children who rebel against this education. It is possible that our collective consciousness makes the Sidhe willing to fit into society without resistance. It is rewarding because there is a lot of joy and happiness in our world, and there is much love. We love our children, and our children feel loved, following without resistance the education system in a way that suits that particular child. I understand that you would like your education to be more attuned to individual needs of the child. Maybe this is not really possible given the higher number of children in your society.

Their pause gave me an opportunity to respond.

POSSIBLE IMPROVEMENTS FOR HUMAN EDUCATION

I understand that it is different to educate the large number of children in our world compared to the small groups that the Sidhe have. To change our education system, we need creativity. As long as we keep holding on to the form of the school as it is now, we will be stuck in an education system that is directed more to the masses than tailored to individuals.

There are many solutions and some have been tried. This is not the place to discuss all possible different education systems in our world. The purpose is to see what we can learn from each other to see what can be changed. To create a new consciousness, one area that needs change is the human education system. Ultimately, we would like to move into a new way of being in this world where both Sidhe and humans live together.

I have a view that I wish could be explored more deeply in human society. I believe that true learning comes from being both a student *and* a teacher. In our education system, we separate these two, creating a structure in which the teacher has all the power and the student has none, or if they are lucky, they have been given limited power in certain schools. I believe that being a teacher and being a student is inseparable. If we can see ourselves as always being both, we continue to grow and expand. This might help us to break free from the confinement of the morphogenetic grid.

A way to do this is by having children teach while they are still students. There would be more teachers making it possible to provide more individual attention to students, which can help address each student's uniqueness. Children would learn many skills as well as how to respect each other. Children would learn to experience their unique qualities and to cultivate what resonates for them. The Sidhe were silent for a while before they responded.

We understand your point of not making this into a discussion about finding solutions for the education of the human race. Your suggestion, however, comes very close to what actually happens in our world. When we mentioned that a child would go to a person that from their perspective was the best person for them to go to, we did not mention that this person might be of any age. We see children preferring other children for exploring and training in certain qualities.

Within our society, that is quite common. You could say that for us the whole community is a school. We believe that this is the only way to optimally develop all skills that are needed to function in our world. Given the way you have set up your society, this will not be accomplished easily. However, your suggestion to allow and encourage children to be the teachers of other children has many qualities that appeal to our Sidhe way of looking at the world.

I understood what the Sidhe shared about children learning from the members of the community to become functional members of the society and world. They also mentioned some roles that Sidhe have. For example, Sha and Ki are both observers. When we desire to acquire a certain function or to do a certain kind of work, we have special schools or universities train us in the skills needed for that function. I wondered how this took place in the Sidhe world.

That is not very different from the way in which children are trained in general to become good members of our society. We go to an individual or a number of individuals to learn the skills needed for the work we would like to do. However, there are no exams. At a certain moment, based on the feedback and based on how we feel about ourselves, we know when we are ready to start with the work we would like to do. We trust that we will also learn through experience when we do the work we have chosen.

If we listen to your stories and what you show us telepathically, we can say that our society is far simpler, more loving, and more respectful, and it has more freedom and is much more relaxed. We do not have competition, which seems to be an inherent part in all areas of your world. We do have problems that come up in our world, but they always get resolved very quickly. Because of the depth of our connections, we will always know whether the issue is truly resolved.

Your world, on the other hand, is very complex, definitely has a lack of freedom, has many rules, and is extremely competitive, which motivates the school system to train people to be competitive. By giving rewards and by having exams, you create differences among people that might have an effect on them for the rest of their lives.

This is especially true because you give value to the differences in results. When you have higher grades, you are "better" than those with lower grades.

Now we better understand why you started your introduction to your education system in a critical way. We feel much compassion for the children who suffer because of your current education system.

I could feel their genuine compassion, and it brought tears to my eyes. The Sidhe are a compassionate and loving people who truly care for other beings. This time I felt these feelings on a much deeper level.

SPECIAL NEEDS

I had one last question in regard to the subject of education that related to children who are born so different that they do not fit in the standard school system. Depending on the country and society, there are special schools or homes for these children. I wondered whether the Sidhe world also had children who did not fit into their society.

I noticed their usual delay in response. I was suddenly aware that the reason for the delay was not that they hesitated in answering a question. They were communicating with other Sidhe. I realized that the communication in its direct form was through Sha and Ki, but in reality, there was a true communication with other Sidhe as well, most likely with their community.

Yes, you are correct. Although we are the contact people, it is our community that is involved in giving the answers or sharing our perspectives. This is done to ensure that what is shared feels correct and is imparted in a way that is in alignment with the general Sidhe consciousness. As individuals, we are not always the right ones to answer the questions you ask or to share about a certain subject. By involving the whole community, we feel that the information is as accurate as is possible, given the limitations that still exist in the communication between us.

We need to say that we are more than surprised and very happy with what we have achieved so far in our communications. This is not only our opinion but also our community's.

Let us address your question: We do not have the same kinds of severe problems as some children experience in your world. All children born have the ability to become well-functioning members of our society. We believe that this largely has to do with the fact that we have a sacred ritual that ensures as much as possible that the characteristics of the child born will be such that the child will function well within our world. This is one of the reasons that our society has so much stability.

The pain and sadness of having a child with physical or mental problems is difficult for us to imagine. It is one of the challenges you are experiencing in your society. We are aware that your society often insufficiently supports parents with, what you call, problem children. This is so difficult for us to understand and can be seen as one of the many barriers between our two races.

So many horrible things happen to children and adults in your world that we have believed your race was a disaster to the system that you call Gaia. We are now aware that an increasing number of people are changing and becoming different from the general patterns of your society. Our exchange about the subject of education has helped us to better understand that it is not easy for human beings to find peace within themselves and within the world.

I felt gratitude that each exchange seemed to contribute to a softening of the judgment of the Sidhe toward humans. There is still a long way to go before judgment is diminished enough to make a more open exchange possible. I do not see that the horrible things people do to each other will suddenly stop. I also do not see our education system suddenly changing. I do see, however, a growing group searching for change, love, and ways to reconnect. I believe that this group of people will be the ones able to cocreate a new reality with the Sidhe and contribute to the fulfillment of the purpose of both races on Earth. This will change Gaia as a whole as well. My sharing with the Sidhe is giving me a growing confidence that we truly can create this new consciousness.

CHAPTER 9

RELATIONSHIPS WITH PLANTS AND ANIMALS

In previous exchanges with Sha and Ki, the focus was mainly for us to have better mutual understanding, which we addressed by sharing the function of our respective worlds. Certainly more could have been shared regarding this subject. However, there were other subjects of equal interest, for example, relationships with other beings and worlds within the Gaia system. After all, our aspiration is to identify ways to raise the vibration of the Gaia system.

We recognize that achieving this goal requires us to see the world as one. We human beings are far from being able to live from this perspective. We see other beings on this planet as enemies (pests, weeds) as food (meat, fruits, vegetables), as a focus for sport (hunting, fishing), as a means of making money (large-scale deforesting, genetic modifications), and fortunately, also as enjoyment (gardening, bird watching, being in nature). Our way of looking at other beings living on this planet reflects the nature of our relationship with Gaia as a whole: Although we can enjoy her beauty to a certain degree, we mainly use her.

We rely on plants and animals as sources of food. I assumed that the Sidhe also eat in some way; therefore, I wished to explore the relationships with plants and animals in our respective worlds. When I indicated my desire to talk about this subject, I felt their openness. I also felt the usual invitation to share first.

I still have mixed feelings about my sharing first in our exchanges.

This was partly because there were so many things I could share and that what I chose to share would influence the process and nature of our mutual sharing. Nonetheless, I found it difficult to say no. I also realized that it helped me to focus better on the subject, and I felt that it helped the Sidhe to answer appropriately.

HUMAN CONNECTION WITH NATURE

From the beginning of time, humans have relied on plants and animals as food; as materials to create protection, such as clothing and housing; and for healing, such as plant medicine. For many people, this dependency on plants and animals generated a deep respect and gratitude for these gifts that made human life possible. It invited humans to connect deeply so as to understand animal behavior and the kind of gifts these animals possess.

This dependency also helped humans to connect with plants and trees to become informed as to how they could best help with food, health, and healing. So initially, there was a realization in human society that nature needed to be respected because it was the source of their survival and proper functioning. There was also a deep connection with nature. People took only what they needed, never more, and accepted a stewardship of nature.

As human society became more complex, an increasingly large part of society no longer connected with nature. People obtained what they needed through trade and later through what is called money, a material that is used to indicate the value of what you had to offer. With this growing disconnection, there was also an increasing desire to have more than what was needed. It was called abundance. It created a society in which people have or have not.

Taking more than what was needed to live a healthy, abundant life was the beginning of the downfall of humans. Obtaining food was no longer based on knowing nature but on making a living. Consequently, people began to look for ways to make production more efficient. Humans wanted to be better than nature, seeing nature as inefficient, which resulted in the development of agriculture, developing plant races and methods of efficiency to produce high volumes of products. The fight against nature began, and balance was lost. It was no longer acceptable that other creatures used what you had planted to sell for your own survival and profit.

Another method of ensuring that there would be enough food was the development of husbandry. People began to keep animals for food and other uses, initially for themselves and later for sale. They created more efficient breeds of cows, pigs, goats, and chickens to produce an abundant supply of milk, eggs, and meat for sale. Animals changed from living beings to production systems, and the respect and love for them began to disappear. These production animals are often kept in horrible living conditions to produce as much as possible with a minimum of monetary expense. In human society, the lives of other beings lost real meaning. Many who say that they love animals eat meat and do not want to know how it got on their tables.

Humans developed other methods to grow an abundant supply of crops. Genetically modified crops were created to have production advantages so that more money could be made. This was done without looking at the consequences. Other plants were viewed as producers of chemical substances to make medications that were sold for lots of money. It was no longer about the gift of a plant and the use of the plants as a whole but about chemical components. These chemical products were isolated or were reproduced artificially. People who take these chemicals often do not know what they are ingesting let alone know where they came from originally. They simply believe that they need to take them to be healthy.

LIVING IN HARMONY WITH NATURE

There are people who realize that we have disconnected from nature and search for ways to reconnect. Most people enjoy nature and the beauty of flowers. There are many animals they enjoy (as long as they are not scary, dangerous, or creepy-crawlies). Many people go on vacation to enjoy nature. Rarely do they really connect with nature on a deeper level. Liking to be in nature is wonderful, but it is not enough. We need a deeper connection and an awareness of our relationship with plants and animals on such a level that we see them again as our relatives on a planet that we share. There is a lot that needs to happen before we are there, but every step we make is a step in the right direction.

I believe that the changes in attitude toward nature should start early and actually should be part of education. We are far from this aspiration. I asked Sha and Ki how the Sidhe see plants and animals in their world, and whether they also use them for food.

The Sidhe have communicated with other human beings, but we have not heard such a critical attitude toward their own species as you have while at the same time expressing a willingness to see what can be done to make changes. We also better understand why you have put so much emphasis on the shift from being connected to the morphogenetic grid to the morphogenetic field. Based on all that is shared, we understand why you see that as the only real solution. The grid of human beings holds so many patterns and behaviors that any change from within the grid might be a very lengthy process if possible at all.

We would like to share that we will do everything we can to support humankind or at least support those who are willing to make that shift. In the meantime, every small positive change will contribute to the whole and might make the shift easier for those people who want to reconnect to the field. This will also help alleviate some of the pain in your world.

As you might understand by now, our world is quite different. The main reason for that is that we are less physical, and also, our longer life span might play a role. We begin to increasingly understand the drives humans have. It seems that the fact that you are physical and that your lives are so short makes it more important for you to have all the comfort and wealth that you believe you need. The Sidhe are, however, amazed that this need to have is so big that people are willing to kill each other over it. But let us address your question.

Yes, we have plants and animals in our world. From our perspective, our world is very beautiful and harmonious. With pride, we would like to share that we see this as our creation and as a reflection of who the Sidhe are. It is important to realize that the same is true for your world. It is a reflection of the consciousness of humankind. Or maybe it is better to say that your world reflects the degree of consciousness that you hold. The lack of connection that humanity has with the world it lives in has alienated it from the very world it lives in.

As much as we create harmony between us, we also create harmony with every living species living in our world. We have telepathic communication with animals, and we are able to communicate with plants. There are people in your world who have this ability. In the past, this used to be quite common in your world. Much of the knowledge of the aboriginal cultures was obtained in this way simply by communication. Plants and animals are very willing to communicate when they feel safe. Of course, there must be a basis for communication, which is lacking in almost all humans.

Because our bodies are not so physical, we do not need physical food. That does not mean that we never take food from plants and trees that are offered to us. We eat fruits because we know that this is a gift, and we eat them in gratitude. We also use certain plants. This depends on many factors.

We do not need them to heal in the way you do. We need them to be able to create certain abilities in a more optimal way. This is different from what you do with plant substances that you use for heightening or expanding your consciousness. You let it happen to you after the plant is prepared according to certain traditions. We do not use plants in this way. We literally collaborate, using the consciousness of the plant and our consciousness, to create a different state of awareness that will allow us to understand something that we need for the community or for our personal functioning to be able to support the community.

We never take animal products. Our system does not need it, and we would not be able to kill an animal for any reason. For us, animals are beings with whom we share the world we live in. We literally cocreate the world. Together, we create a stable world. We have no species in our world that disrupt our harmony and balance. The fact that you have such animals is a reflection of your consciousness.

We are aware of your stories of paradise. Initially, when both our races were still one, there was paradise. All living species within the Gaia system were living together harmoniously. It might sound like a fairy tale, but it was reality then. The world was never created to be disharmonious.

When we arrived as the new species, we were given the ability to cocreate and explore what cocreation meant in this world. When the decision was made by our ancestors to separate from those who went deeper into physicality, we still had the ability to be cocreators on the level of consciousness that you would call oneness. In those days, nothing was solid and definitely not as solid as it is nowadays in your world. Therefore, the plants and animals were also more etheric in appearance. In our world, they still are. You would not recognize them as anything with which you are familiar because they changed within our world to be able to maintain the harmony within the world we created. We literally feed each other to stay in balance and in harmony.

An aspect of education that we did not yet mention is the training to live in harmony with all creatures in our world. As you descended into lower physical vibration, all the plants and animals in your world did that as well. As you created disharmony within your world, this disharmony was also reflected in the animals and even the plants in your world. This has contributed to the belief that the outside world is your enemy. As your consciousness begins to change, so will the world you live in.

I knew that they were right. I have written about this in one of my books. Our consciousness changes weather patterns, induces earthquakes and eruptions of volcanoes, and affects nature in many ways.[1] It is very important that people become aware that our collective consciousness has the power to disrupt systems, as we are killed through disasters as a consequence of our own way of being. We need this understanding on a large scale in order for this to change. This understanding and awareness can help people realize that it is important for us to take responsibility for all of our emotions, thoughts, and behaviors.

BONDING WITH ANIMALS AND PLANTS

It is important for us to realize that most everything we think, feel, say, or do is fear based. With that knowledge, we can learn methods to change these patterns. A growing number of people have begun to make these changes. These changes are also now reflected in the behavior of animals. We are seeing an increase in the special bonds between humans and animals and between species of animals that previously would not be together. These are promising signs.

This brought up another question: We have pets who live with us. The most common pets are cats and dogs, but there are also many types of rodents and even reptiles, amphibians, and spiders kept as pets. From what I heard from the Sidhe, it is very unlikely that they have pets. Therefore, I wanted to know whether the Sidhe develop special bonds with particular animals.

It is true that we do not hold pets as you do. We do understand the longing for having animals close to you. We believe that it reflects the subconscious memories of being with animals in a harmonious way, as we have in our world. With very few exceptions, pets are not threatening; therefore, the love for animals that is still built into the human system can be expressed freely. However, from our perspective, it is impossible to hold pets in the same way as humans do. Having animals locked up in an apartment, in a cage, or putting them on a leash is something we would not be able to do. So in that sense and according to your definition, we do not have pets.

However, there are special bonds between Sidhe and animals. These bonds are developed in a natural way based on a mutual attraction that you might call a resonance of energies. These bonds are personal and can develop between Sidhe and a large variety of animals. These animals visit whenever the animal feels like it. Also, a Sidhe might visit an animal in the area where it lives.

Most Sidhe have telepathic connections with a variety of animals. Therefore, we can "call" each other to see whether there is the possibility and the space for both the Sidhe and the animal to connect. Some of these bonds are quite intimate and can stretch over many years.

Connecting with animals is part of our children's education. Connecting with plants and trees is also included. Because we have a deep respect for all life, the training to properly connect and interact with plants and animals is an important part of education and is an inherent part of the Sidhe life.

When we eat the fruits of the plants and trees, we do this because it is offered to us. You might not call this eating because neither the Sidhe nor the fruits are physical. However, from our perspective, we take the fruit in and thus eat it. Fruits are gifts that we accept in gratitude. We never kill a plant for food. From our perspective and way of living, there is no need for that.

In some very rare instances, we use parts of a plant but never to the degree that a plant dies from it. We are aware that you need to have plants to simply survive. Our main sustenance is life force, which is abundantly present everywhere. We have developed ways to take in life force without needing any living being to do that for us.

From our perspective, we live in the paradise that you know from stories. Many people doubt whether that story is really true. We would like to share with you that it is true: We live in it.

Paradise — it sounds so wonderful. It has always been a dream of mine to be able to communicate with animals, plants, and trees. In this phase of my life, I have developed only some limited skills. It would be wonderful to have the skills of the Sidhe. Their lives really sound wonderful, and I fully understand that they do not want to give that up.

Would I like to have a life as they describe, realizing that for me it would be a dream come true? As tempting as it might be, the answer is no. Feeling deeper into it, I can see the beauty, but I also see something else. I see that the Sidhe, like us, are locked up in their matrix. And no matter how wonderful the matrix, it is still a prison. I do not want to exchange one prison for another. I long for freedom from any prison, even from the most beautiful one. I enjoy the sharing from the Sidhe, and through their sharing, I can feel the beauty of their world. However, I will continue to find ways to get out of the grid that I am locked into to make it possible to express in the fullest way feasible who I truly am. That is the true joy that I long for.

THE HAWTHORN AND THE MANZANITA

I have read, according to the Celtic traditions, that there is a special connection between the Sidhe and the Hawthorn tree. When I mentioned this to a person who has a deep connection with plants and trees, she felt that this could mean that the connection of the Sidhe in the Southwest of the United States could be with the Manzanita. I wondered whether there was any truth to this.

The Celtic people had a special connection with trees. For the Celtic people, trees were their allies and symbols of different aspects of power. They used the energies of the trees to help them in basically every aspect of their lives. The way they saw the energies and spirits of plants and trees has changed over time. Consciousness, as well as the energies of plants, has changed.

To honor the Sidhe with whom they were connecting, they selected a specific tree to express that honor. They felt that the energies of the Hawthorn held aspects that they associated with their experiences of the connections they felt with the Sidhe. That is why the idea of a relationship between the Sidhe and the Hawthorn tree has entered the consciousness of humankind. From that perspective, and based on certain qualities of these two shrubs, we understand how an association between the Hawthorn and Manzanita can be made.

When the ancestors of the Sidhe were creating the Sidhe world, they made choices. From a human perspective, you might think that these choices were exaggerated. There was a strong feeling that to create a harmonious world certain things would not fit. One of the things that would not fit is plants and trees having spikes and thorns. Those attributes are used to defend themselves against predators. Our ancestors created a world with a vibration in which there was no need for these attributes. Therefore, we do not have a Hawthorn as you have in your world. It simply does not fit within the consciousness that has been created and maintained in our world.

This confirmed the idea of paradise once more. Living in the Southwest of the United States, I meet many plants with thorns, spikes, hooks, or razor-sharp leaves. I could live in a world that does not have this. I am very aware that these attributes fit within the consciousness of our world, like a reflection of the need to defend oneself and harm others in the process. Even so, I still do not choose to live in a paradise prison. I would rather explore the possibilities that a new consciousness could bring to this world.

CHAPTER 10

CRYSTALLINE ENERGIES

I wanted to talk to the Sidhe about an important subject in my life, and I felt that this was the right moment. The Sidhe knew how important this was for me and were excited to share with me, asking me again to introduce the subject. I accepted gladly, as this had become our usual approach.

THE VALUE OF CRYSTALLINE ENERGY

I would like to start with a statement because many people forget or might not even be aware: Planet Earth is a crystalline expression of the consciousness of Gaia. Earth can be defined as a giant crystalline system. Within this system, all kinds of processes take place that create and change these crystalline structures. While we are learning about these structures, we encounter an increasing amount of diversity in forms and energies. From my perspective, Earth itself is a dynamic crystalline system.

When most people think of crystalline forms, they think of crystals that are either in their raw form or cut and polished. We have learned that all these different crystalline systems are beautiful and that they also radiate energies that we are now beginning to understand. Because of the diversity of their energies, crystals are considered by many people as important tools on the journey of expanding consciousness.

Crystals seem to have been used for ages. It seems their beauty has always fascinated people, especially certain types called gemstones. Consequently, we have given them value, which has led to theft, crime, and killings — which unfortunately seem to be inevitable attributes of human behavior. All these negative behaviors are based on the value seen from a physical perspective. Although most people look at the monetary value of crystals, far fewer people look at their energetic values. For those who are on their spiritual paths and for those who use crystals for healing, it is important to look at the energies of crystals and stones. Whole systems have been developed to train people in the art of using crystalline energies for healing.

I believe that the crystals and stones energetic qualities are their main value. The more I learn, the less I know. Their energies are complex, and because I am speaking from a physical perspective, I am aware that there are many energies and qualities of which I am unaware or hardly aware.

CRYSTAL SKULLS

When I began to study crystals, I came across an interesting phenomenon that has kept me studying since my first encounter. The phenomenon is crystal skulls. The crystal skull legend that has become part of my belief structure begins in ancient times. In those times, there were no such things as crystal skulls. Rather, there was a connection between twelve star nations who transmitted information to humankind. The information was intended to be integrated into the consciousness of the human species in such a way as to assist humans to fulfill their purpose: to become true caretakers of all expressions of Gaia and to bring the frequencies of the Gaia system to such a level that ascension of the Gaia system as a whole would take place. This was also the purpose of the ancestors of the Sidhe and humans, and it might suggest that this information was also intended for the Sidhe and could be part of your history. Of course, I would love to hear your response.

Human beings were indeed going deeper into the material physical density that prevented them from connecting fully with the information that the star nations had given them. So the star nations invited those who were still connected to create a storage system for this information. It needed to be a natural, basically indestructible, and easily recognizable storage device — hence, we have the crystal skulls made of quartz crystals.

Quartz has a great storage capacity. Being a great connector, it can easily help to connect with a field of information. The shape of the human skull is a symbol that helps humans to remember that this is a storage device of information that needs to be processed. Human beings process information with their brains in order to arrive at awareness. An interesting aspect is that when the ancient people created crystal skulls, they created them in a way that the shape adds an energy system to the energy of the materials from which they were made. These additional energies help us human beings to expand our consciousnesses and our abilities in many ways. They can help us expand our consciousnesses to such a degree that we might be able to access the information held within the crystal skulls; thus, we will be able to fulfill our purpose on Earth.

With all of my passion for this subject and having written two books about crystal skulls,[1] I am still far from accessing the information that either is in or connected with the crystal skulls. I have always wondered why it seems so challenging to connect with this information.

Based on earlier sharing, I wondered whether it could be possible that the field of information of crystal skulls might be connected to the morphogenetic field and not to the morphogenetic grid. This could be the reason that we still cannot easily access the information connected with crystal skulls. The information might be encoded in the crystalline matrix with such a high vibration that only those who are able to enter the morphogenetic field can access the information in the crystal skulls.

The other possibility is that the information in the crystal skulls can only be accessed when the crystal skulls are brought into a high vibrational state. We might still not be able to bring the crystal skulls to the right vibrational state to access the information connected with them.

CRYSTALLINE LIFE FORCE

I am aware that crystalline energies are very important within the system that we call our world. Our technologies are destroying the natural crystalline grid systems.[2] My feeling is that this induces limitations in the energetic and spiritual development of human beings and could prevent the development and raising of the vibrations of the whole Gaia system. Although some people are aware of ways to create aspects of crystalline grids that can take over the natural functions of disappearing grids, this is only happening on a small scale.[3]

The destruction of the crystalline grids in cities and towns may be one of the reasons why so many people feel disconnected from Earth. We see the disconnection from Earth more strongly in people who live in cities where the crystalline grids no longer exist.

I was aware I was giving a very limited overview. I hoped that the Sidhe's ability to read beyond the words would give them a sufficient basis to start the sharing.

As always, we thank you for your willingness to be the one who introduces the subject. We always learn a lot because getting glimpses of how you see the subject brings our understanding beyond what we have gathered over time from the human beings we have observed. It gives us a better feeling for what may be important to share as part of creating a deeper understanding between our two races.

Thanks to our interactions, we realize that among humans, the understanding of energies is much higher than what we were aware of. We also feel that energy systems might be a subject that can bring us closer to each other. You might understand that we are also pleasantly surprised about your awareness of the star nations that gave information to the human race. But before coming to that, let us start with your beginning statement of Earth being a crystalline being.

By now, you are very aware that we are not focused on any physical aspect; therefore, we also are not focused on the physical aspects of crystals. We understand your term "crystalline beings" well, though. The energetic patterns of crystals and crystalline structures are very different from that of plants and animals. However, they also have similarities. The similarities are that we consider them all alive. For us, crystals are also alive, and so is Earth. Crystals and Earth have a life force of which human beings are hardly aware.

At this point I interrupted. In our workshops, we had worked with this life force. We call it the crystalline life force because it feels like more of a basic life force that supports all other living beings. We had noticed, however, that not all crystals and stones have this life force. In collaboration with Mother Earth, this life force can be brought into the crystals and stones. We discovered that there is a sacred stone from India that holds the crystalline life force more strongly than other stones. We call these stones Shiva lingams (see image 10.1). The Sidhe then responded.

Image 10.1:
A Shiva lingam.

You are correct. That is indeed the life force to which we are referring. In our world, this life force is powerfully present, and it supports all life. As you have noticed, there are many stones and crystals in your world that either do not or hardly hold the life force. There are two reasons for this. The first one is that they have been disconnected from the source of this life force, Earth, in a way that made it impossible for them to hold the life force they had. This has to do with the greed you were referring to and reflects the lack of respect for these crystalline beings.

Crystals are mined in almost all cases without love and respect. That forces the crystals to lose what little life force they have. All of this is the consequence of human disconnection from the whole and their resulting ignorance that crystalline beings are alive.

We say "little life force" because that is what we experience. As we are beginning to better understand the dynamics between our worlds, we have to say with some hesitance and some shame that we are beginning to recognize the reason for that. When the two groups began to separate, initially there was still one world.

The Sidhe ancestors wanted to create their own world separate from those going deeper into the material realm because they believed that this was the only way to maintain their state of consciousness and high vibrations. We have by now mentioned this many times. To enable this to happen, they began to pull higher vibrational energies into what you call a matrix, which we understand now is what you call a morphogenetic grid. When we became more powerful, we pulled more and more energy into the system to allow us to maintain our high vibrational state.

However, we were pulling energy away from somewhere. Of course, the only place we could pull it away from was what you call your world, the world from which we separated. In a sense, this was devastating. The more powerful our world became, the weaker yours became. We accelerated the process of your descent into the physical material world to the point that the life force diminished significantly in your world. We are like those who hoard precious metals and gemstones in your world, but we did it with life force.

Mind you, we were not aware of these consequences. Our ancestors were too focused on maintaining their vibrational state. Looking at it now, they might have pulled out of your system more than they really needed. This is the background for many issues in your world, like short life spans and, as you mentioned, a low amount of life force. Your behavior only makes it worse. By polluting your world, the life force is decreasing even more, and the increasing population contributes to the problem.

Because you are locked up in your morphogenetic grid, your consciousness maintains a situation that insufficiently changes. You already mentioned that in collaboration with Earth, life force can be brought back into your world. That seems to be an important way to improve the situation in your world.

The Sidhe went silent for a while. I could feel their sadness for what had happened. Both the Sidhe and humans have made many mistakes in the past. I am not a person who likes to dwell in the past. For me, there is only the now moment, and in each now moment, there is an opportunity for new choices.

EARTH'S VIBRATIONS SUPPORT ALL LIVING BEINGS

After the Sidhe's sharing, I saw in my mind a solution that seemed optimal. The two worlds needed to merge and integrate again. I was immediately aware that this solution would not be seen as practical, and the Sidhe most likely would not see this as being very desirable, but it ultimately seemed to be the most optimal way to carry out our common goal of raising the vibration of Gaia.

> We understand your point, and you might be right. Given the tremendous differences between the two races, this approach will not be possible in the near future. Whether or not it will be possible further in the future will all depend on what will be achieved by those who are willing to explore the collaboration between our two races. We feel that this is the priority of the communication and collaboration that we are establishing right now.

I anticipated that response, but I at least wanted to mention what seems like a logical approach. It is not important what I as an individual would like to see happen. What is important is mutual love and respect for each other and to find ways that work for our respective races. By now, the Sidhe might understand that I like to challenge. But I wanted to go back to the crystalline energies. We agreed that crystalline material holds life force. Next, I wanted to know how the Sidhe work with the crystalline energies.

> As we explained, the primary function of crystalline energies is their life force that supports our world. The crystalline energies are the basis for our paradise. In essence, we see Earth as the provider of the life force needed for all life. In addition, Earth's vibrations support all living beings with everything that is needed. These two groups of energies, the life force and the more specific energies, provide all that we need. Therefore, we do not need physical food in our world

as you need in yours. This is true for all species in our world: the life force and the specific energies are all that is needed.

That immediately raised my interest. There are people who call themselves breatharians. They claim that they can live on life force alone. My feeling has always been that this is not really 100 percent possible. Feeling into it, I started to believe that it might be possible to get all the energies that we need from Earth. Listening to the Sidhe, it seemed that this is what they were saying.

You are correct again. This is what we are saying. We are aware that there are people who are exploring this approach. However, this is only possible when your energy system has enough purity to enable it to connect and resonate with the energies that are needed. You need to be permanently plugged in, so to speak. It is an attunement, a state of connection based on awareness that only very few human beings can achieve in this moment. It means that you have to dis-connect from all that is physical, including from the physical body's reaction to what it believes it needs.

Your systems are programmed to eat. To wean your body off the program that solid food is needed is challenging because there is no collective support. In addition, pollution makes it more diffi-cult. The fact that the supportive energies in your world are so much weaker than in our world makes the challenge in your world even higher. In our world, everything supports this way of living. For us, it is as natural as it is for you to eat. However, if you truly can live that way, your lives would be prolonged tremendously.

When we talk about our food being the specific energies from Earth that we need, we are actually talking about minerals, metals, and crystals. We are talking about their energies and their qualities that we connect with and take in. We possess a very extensive knowl-edge about the energetic qualities of crystals, minerals, and metals and also about how to connect with these energies. This is what we teach our children.

At first, we need to help the children make this connection so that they have all they need to grow and develop in a healthy way.

The way we do this is by energy blending. In this way, we can feel what a child needs. We then connect with the required energies so that the child is fed. It also makes it possible for the child to learn to feel the energies and to connect. Over time, children learn to do this by themselves. As adults, we always help each other when some of the connections are not clear or powerful enough. You can compare that with checking whether a person gets all he or she needs in his or her food, including minerals and vitamins.

Listening to what they shared, I could only conclude that we do not even have a basic knowledge of what minerals, metals, and crystals can do for us. They agreed.

You are very physically oriented, so you always look at what is lacking on a physical level. That is very important for your well-being. However, you either are not aware or are hardly aware that you also need certain energies to maintain balance in your etheric and astral bodies. When there was still harmony in nature and your food sources came from a place of harmony, all these needs were reasonably well fulfilled. This is no longer the case. Hardly anybody in your world gets the energies that are needed for your other two physical bodies: the etheric and the astral.

With the increasing breakdown of your world, this may even get worse. From our perspective, the main reason for your short lives is the lack of these energies. The improvements in your medical field have added a couple of decades, but not centuries, to your lives. Without a deeper understanding of the energetic needs of the etheric and astral bodies, that further extension of your lives will never be achieved.

I had to ask: Is this something that the Sidhe could teach us? Obviously, this was one of those questions that required consultation within the community.

Among us, there is a willingness to do that. However, in this moment and phase of our sharing, we do not know how to do this. Energies cannot be fully expressed in words. The way we teach this subject is through a combination of blending and telepathic communication. We are unable to blend with you, and the telepathic communication only works in this phase with respect to general subjects.

Even in the general subjects, we both experience moments in which we cannot proceed or where there simply is no clear transmission. This is one of the subjects that we need to add to the list for the future. We are sorry about this. We wish we could help you with this, as this would be a major step forward in bringing the two races together.

I could feel their genuine longing to help us. If there was one subject of which I would like to improve our communication, it would be this one.

STAR SYSTEM CONNECTIONS

I did not want to end the discussion about crystalline energies without hearing whether they had something to say on the subject of crystal skulls.

As you might understand, we do not have any connection with physical crystal skulls. In all honesty, we were hardly aware of their existence and never really looked into this subject. We believe that this is a rather unique aspect in human history. However, what interested us is the part of your story that refers to information that has been given to the people of Earth as part of a support system for their evolution.

Interestingly, according to those who hold the history of the Sidhe, there is a similar story about information from the star nations. However, this does not get much attention in our world. Most likely, this might be because this story was from before the separation. After the separation, the focus has been on creating the world of the Sidhe. That does not mean that we are not connecting with the star systems. To the contrary, we talked about that before. We actually see connecting with the star systems as a way to maintain the essence of who we are. If we understand you correctly, the information from the star nations you talk about is not so much about where you came from, your origins, but more about helping you as a species to fulfill a purpose.

We have to admit that the Sidhe as a race do not have a purpose other than to maintain the essence of who we think we are, or maybe we should say, who we think we need to be. You can call it arrogance, but we believe that we know who we are. We see human beings as the ones who do not know who they are. We are beginning to understand that what we have done is created an image of who we thought we needed to be, and we are still holding on to that image.

When we connect with the star systems, it is mainly to be supported in holding on to the image of the ideal Sidhe. This might explain why we no longer connect with certain star systems. These star systems contribute insufficiently to supporting our system; therefore, we no longer need a connection with them.

As I mentioned, the crystal skulls are connected to twelve different star systems. I have spent only a limited amount of time on a limited region of what I know is an area where the Sidhe live. I found five portals in that area. Two of them belong to the group of twelve that we have connected to the crystal skulls: Sirius and what we call Ursa Major.

As was mentioned earlier, I did not feel a connection between the Sidhe and Sirius, but there was a connection with Ursa Major. I also felt a connection with the Sidhe to Pegasus, Antares, and Spica, a star in the constellation of Virgo. These last three systems have no relationship with crystal skulls of which I am aware. We might be able to learn about the connections the Sidhe have with star systems by looking at the portals to which the Sidhe are connected. It seemed to me that their connection with star systems do not have much in relation to crystal skulls.

There was one of those long pauses in our connection. For a moment, I had the feeling that they were unhappy I had this knowledge. I had a similar feeling when I used the morphogenetic grid of the Sidhe in the beginning to connect with them. Was this information too direct and too close?

There is surprise among the Sidhe about your ability to already have some knowledge about our connections with the stars. However, we are also aware that you do not understand the energetic meaning of the connections we have. We are not ready to share these aspects of our essence yet.

By mentioning the words "too close," you are right. We have lived totally separated from humans. When we connected, it was to help or support you in specific situations. It has been a long time since a human has been so closely aware of those energies that we consider to be Sidhe. You challenge us more than we anticipated. It is something that we have to get used to. We feel complete with this subject for now.

They might have been surprised, but so was I. I mentioned earlier that I knew about their connections with some star systems. However, I did not feel that I knew much about these star systems. The little that I did know was that they had a connection with certain star systems, but I did not know what that meant. Even if I knew more, my intention would never be to invade their sacred space. This means that to the best of my ability, I will never do something without their permission. There remains much to learn before we are more focused on collaboration instead of being surprised about what we know and what we do not know.

CHAPTER 11

SUBTLE WORLDS

There was a major subject that I wanted to talk about with the Sidhe. It is another subject that has been very important in my life. Throughout the years, it has been considered fantasy in the human world, but now it is viewed as an area of exploration. This subject is subtle worlds. From a certain perspective, the Sidhe could be seen as being part of the subtle worlds. Others, knowing that the Sidhe and we have common ancestors, do not place the Sidhe in the subtle worlds. As always, it is a matter of definition. Therefore, it seems appropriate to start with some definitions.

Some of our scientists, like the physicist David Bohm,[1] distinguishes between what is called the manifested world (the explicate order) and the implicate order, in which the energies exist in a state of potential and are "premanifest." Bohm calls the energies of the implicate order subtle energies. We also use the term subtle energies to refer to those energies in our system that we cannot measure. Nonetheless, we believe they exist and know that they can be perceived by senses other than the physical senses. These were mentioned in chapter 6. All of this is part of what humans might call subtle energies.

However, when I talk about subtle worlds, I am referring to those worlds that are part of the earth, invisible to the human senses, and occupied by beings such as nature spirits, dragons, unicorns, elementals, devas, angels, djinn, water beings, and air beings. These beings from the subtle worlds are an inherent part of the Gaia system. Therefore, they are important for us as well, especially when we talk about the responsibility to raise the vibration of the Gaia system. Beings of the subtle worlds might want to share their opinion, vision, and other contributions.

THE CONSEQUENCES OF SEPARATING WORLDS

Among humans, there is an increasing interest in beings from the subtle realms accompanied by a large range of opinions about them. Humans often look at these beings from a human perspective and have the tendency to make them human-like (anthropomorphic vision). We see this reflected in many books and card decks wherein subtle beings have qualities that, in my opinion, do not actually belong to them but rather are known as human qualities.

Because we are looking at ways in which we can help each other to fulfill our roles within the Gaia system, I believe that it is important to share about the subtle worlds. In other books about the Sidhe, it is said that the Sidhe have a connection with the subtle worlds, in particular with nature spirits. The subject of the subtle worlds is so vast that I asked the Sidhe about which aspects they wished to exchange ideas.

We are very happy to discuss the subtle worlds with you. We understand the definitions and descriptions you are using better now than we would have in the initial phase of our sharing. From the perspective of your physical world, there are worlds that you would call subtle, but for us, they are part of our world.

When we go back to the time when our worlds were still one, the worlds that you call subtle worlds were simply an aspect of the reality we lived in. These worlds were all aspects of Gaia that differed only in frequency and in function. There was no separation between these worlds; it was all one functional system. There was respect. There was love.

The feeling of being one system was such that the worlds were one integrated, dynamically interacting whole. You can use the word that brings a smile to your faces: "paradise." We know that it can be difficult for you to imagine that the world was once just like we described.

In the beginning, the beings with different frequency ranges were not yet caught up in seemingly separate systems. All beings could move within the frequency ranges that belonged to their specific characteristics and functions in one dynamic energy system. There was no separation; there was one world in which beings moved around and interacted with others based on their frequency system.

The ancestors of both our races were the only species that could cover all these frequency ranges and therefore could connect with the beings from all vibrational systems. Thus, in the beginning, there were no separate worlds but only one integrated system — one world — Gaia.

When the Sidhe talk about separation, we talk about a decision that is as important for the Sidhe as Independence Day is for the American people. For us, it is the decision that makes us the Sidhe that we are today. It prevented us from moving into the chaos that human beings live in. We have always looked at it as the best decision we could have made. However, sharing with you and others has taught us to see the consequences of separation that we had never looked at before. One of the consequences is the effect that the separation has had on those you call subtle beings.

When we started to create our world, we not only pulled energies into our world but also brought many beings with us. Within Gaia, all beings have a function, creating together the beauty and diversity of Gaia's expression. The different beings are also needed to maintain everything in creation in an optimal state. We see these processes as natural and something in flow. We do not need to know how they work. We only need to know how to flow with these processes and with all beings who contribute to these flows in order to maintain that which feels right. We know how to create new aspects when needed through clear intent and collaboration.

When we created our world to be separate from yours, we also created a separation in the subtle worlds. We know that we did it, but the real impact of the separation was not clear to us. Let us talk about a few groups of subtle beings to help both of us understand what the reality is at this moment as seen from our perspective. This also makes it possible to look at options for potential changes in the future without the need to give up our worlds, assuming that this is achievable. We would like to start with the nature spirits to see what you know about them.

In most cases, I knew immediately what to say. This introduction by the Sidhe touched me more deeply than I had expected. I clearly felt the potential for oneness, and it awakened a deep longing in me. Now that the Sidhe asked me to share about the nature spirits, I was shocked back to reality. I immediately realized how little I actually know about nature spirits. I also felt how much the information from different sources had influenced me. I never felt confident about any aspect of the limited knowledge that I had about nature spirits. I felt that I needed to take a deep breath, refocus, and simply start with my sharing without being worried about my lack of knowledge.

NATURE SPIRITS, ELEMENTALS, DEVAS, AND MORE

For me, nature spirits is a very complex subject. In the past, I have tried to see patterns in the tremendous amount of beings that I, to some degree, can sense. In my attempts to see patterns, I have separated them into three main groups. The first group is the nature spirits who are part of the process of creating the beings that we call crystals, plants, trees, and animals. These nature spirits help with birth, healing, support during growth, and the process of maintenance. They direct the tiny little beings, which I call elementals, who form the second group. I know that defining these elementals as a separate group might be confusing because many people have the tendency to see many nature spirits as elementals.

In earlier chapters, we mentioned that the four elements connected with physical reality are fire, water, air, and earth. These elements are elemental forces and powers. In different traditions, beings are mentioned as guardians of these forces. For example, Archangel Michael is seen as the guardian of the force of fire, Archangel Raphael of water, Archangel Gabriel of air, and Archangel Uriel of Earth. Many native peoples, especially those in the Americas, use power animals as guardians of these forces, and dragons can also be seen this way.

Most people who talk about elements will refer to the physical expressions of the elemental powers. This means they talk about water as a substance, about fire that burns, about air that moves (wind, storms, and hurricanes), and about the earth in which plants grow. Many books have been written about working with these physical elements.[2]

Devas and fairies are believed to be connected with these physical elements and therefore are often called elemental beings. Examples are gnomes connected with earth, sylphs with air, undines with water, and salamanders with fire. However, different authors use the term "elemental beings" for other beings as well. Examples are the dragons who also work with the elemental powers.

Although all these beings are called elemental beings, they work with all four elemental forces while mainly being associated with one of the four elements. The tiny beings that I define as elementals are the most basic spirits that work only with one of the four elemental forces within the different realities, both of a physical or subtle nature. I have not yet encountered any other beings with these characteristics.

The third group of nature spirits is the devas. They are the ones who guard the environment within which the nature spirits and elementals work. This environment can be of any size, from a small object to the size of an ocean. I see the devic world as hierarchical. One deva is not more important than another, but within each system, there is a main deva. There are other devas who work with parts of the system, and each part also has parts that have other devas and so on.

Within the world of nature spirits, there is so much diversity that I would not know where to begin. Every stone, plant, and animal has its own nature spirit and its own deva.

I was very curious about the way the Sidhe saw this system, because I understood that they were able to see nature spirits. Few humans can sense nature spirits and at best have a limited perception of them.

You have helped us to look at the level of awareness of humans in a different way. We apologize for the fact that we have had a tendency to see the human race as being a threat to our society without having the willingness to look at the differences in spiritual development in different people in your world and the degree to which they are aware of what you call the subtle aspects of your world. Your summary about the nature spirits reflects that as well.

We are aware that you naturally approach your description from a physical perspective, but we can only agree with the outline you have given. From our perspective, there are also these main functional groups, the difference being the frequencies with which they work in our world and in yours.

Over and over, we have to go back to the separation. It feels increasingly painful for us to talk about it, realizing all the effects it has had. During the paradise phase of oneness, all beings worked together, each expressing the role he or she was created to fulfill. There was a continuous and harmonious flow of energies.

Shortly before the separation, we observed what we called ripples in these natural harmonious flows. Looking back and looking at it from a human perspective, you might say that these were ripples of change that were necessary for us to fulfill our mutual goal. Now you might say that this was the moment that we needed more than ever to collaborate. However, the opposite happened.

We felt that we needed the separation, and in order to make that separation possible, we needed to bring nature spirits, elementals, and devas into our world. So that is what happened. Therefore, we separated not only the world of the humanoids but also the world of the nature spirits, elementals, and devas. This was not an issue for the elementals, because they exist throughout the physical worlds, subtle or not. The separation had a larger effect on nature spirits and devas.

Nature spirits and devas are very flexible. When the worlds separated, those who stayed with us adjusted to our world, and those who stayed with you adjusted to yours. There are many nature spirits who are now part of your world that would have no place in ours. However, there is a certain degree of exchange possible between the two worlds, and some of the nature spirits move regularly between them.

The main difference is not so much in the types of nature spirits but more in the way we work with them. Because of our deep connection with all that exists in our world, we also have a deep connection with the nature spirits. We cocreate and collaborate to maintain the high quality of our environment, and in that way, our world has a lot of similarities with the original paradise.

One of the ways in which humans can change the world they live in is through reconnecting with nature spirits. When we talk about reconnecting, we do not mean to learn to perceive them and maybe to greet them. We mean to make a deeper connection so that you can begin to understand their work on a deeper level.

Through collaboration, you will be able to change your world for the greater good of all. It will be part of the creation of a new consciousness in which we might be able to begin to bridge our two worlds. We believe that our connections with our respective nature spirits are the key in our two worlds to being able to bridge our differences and to be able to really work together in collaboration. When we talk about nature spirits, we include devas, because we see them as being equally needed for the functioning of nature as a whole.

CONNECTING WITH NATURE SPIRITS

Given their deep connection with nature spirits, I wanted to know what the Sidhe thought was the best approach for us to make the connection, deepen the connection, and guide other human beings to be able to connect with the nature spirits. This question was paramount for me, especially given Sha and Ki's statement that this may be a way to begin to bridge the worlds. I welcomed any suggestions.

You already know the answer. The only way to connect with any being is through love and respect. From that place, you set the intent to connect. You have made many connections in the past. However, these connections were always superficial. That does not work with nature spirits.

Although there are differences, the major approach of a nature spirit is either a full connection or no connection. They are most willing to help you build up the connection, but to collaborate, they want to feel that you are working together fully and equally. Devas are much easier in that respect. They accept more easily what is and are glad for everything that is available.

Because the nature spirit world is such a large and diverse world, it may be wise in the initial phase to find a nature spirit that has energy with whom you can more easily connect and resonate. Once you have an ally in the world of nature spirits, this ally can help you to find your way in that world.

Do not try to connect with many nature spirits at the same time, especially in the beginning. You might never establish a strong connection. We cannot help you with the first contact. That is very personal. Go into your heart and feel around in nature for the nature spirit you might have a resonance with. Once your connection has been established, it will become easier for us to give suggestions.

They were right. I knew the answer. Finding a quick and easy way to accomplish everything we do is a common human quality (this also applies to me). We love to look for the magic pill that will do everything for us. At the same time, I am fully aware that it takes time to establish a contact. This might be even truer for connecting with beings from the subtle realms because it is much vaguer to us than working with physical things. Working with the subtle world is less concrete and can easily lead to fantasies and imagination instead of true connection and perception. However, in an exploration, there are ways that work and ways that do not. We need to learn from both.

I felt at that point the level of sharing about nature spirits was covered sufficiently for the moment. In their sharing about separation, I felt that at the moment of separation, other beings had also been affected. I was curious what the Sidhe were willing to share about the many other subtle worlds.

THE DJINN

I felt that the subjects the Sidhe considered difficult always created longer pauses because they either did not know all the aspects or they did not want to share. During these pauses, I am sure they had telepathic conversations among the Sidhe at a frequency to which I have no access. For whatever reasons, the subject of other subtle realms and beings seemed uncomfortable, probably because it had to do with the consequences of the separation.

You are really beginning to understand us. Yes, it has to do with the separation. So far, we have shared that it also meant a certain degree of separation in the world of the nature spirits. This has not created many challenges, because the temperament of nature spirits is to simply do what they feel they need to do. However, there are many other subtle realms with beings who have different functions and roles that were not very clear at the moment of separation.

The ancestors of the Sidhe made a selection and decided which subtle beings were allowed and which were not accepted in our newly developing world. At that time, this approach was so much a part of our consciousness that it felt the right thing for us to do. It never came up in our awareness to ask whether that really was true. It is only through deeper connections with human beings that these questions are now arising.

There are subtle worlds that, although part of the original world, are now only part of yours and not of ours and vice versa. There are also subtle realms that have been part of both worlds for a long time. The beings of these realms are the beings of your fairy tales and fantasies. We are aware that we as Sidhe also play a role in these fantasy stories, often under different names, depending on the role the storyteller seems to think is appropriate for the story.

Many of the subtle worlds and subtle beings simply flowed with the separation. In many cases, it was not clear what consequences they would endure. Most likely, we will never understand what these consequences really were. However, some beings were affected in a way that they considered unpleasant. We have seen some aspects of that, and we have seen that some of these consequences have really affected your race. We refer specifically to the group of subtle beings that you call the djinn. They were not allowed to be part of our world because they felt closer to the physical realms. In addition, their energies were such that they were not desired.

[Note: Djinn are not well known in the Western world, but it seems that they are becoming more common nowadays. They are better known in the Middle East. We know them from stories as the genies in the bottle. They are, however, mostly invisible beings. They make themselves visible as dark shadows on walls and induce a great fear in people. They also can make noise, and some poltergeist phenomena are actually caused by djinn. Djinn are seen as negative spirits, especially in the Middle East but increasingly also in the West. From my perspective, the djinn are a group of beings connected with the element of fire.]

Being in a world that has increased in density along with humans who created what the djinn see as a messed-up world was a reason for the djinn to become adversaries of humans. They apparently blame humans that they are no longer in paradise. The energies kept them out of our world, which made a disturbing factor in your world.

We are aware that you personally do not see the djinn as negative, which in your world is quite exceptional. You see them as very reactive and angry. Their fiery nature makes them behave the way they do. You personally are able to establish a connection with them in which you can make agreements. It is this observation of your connection with the djinn that makes us realize that other choices could have been made.

However, we cannot turn the clock back, and as you know, we Sidhe are not willing to give up our world. Maybe changing your world will make a future reconnection possible. Establishing connections with subtle beings and growing to higher vibrations is a very important part of this process.

I was surprised that the Sidhe were aware of the existence of the djinn. Knowing the energies of the djinn, I thought that the Sidhe would not be aware of them.

I was happy with what the Sidhe shared. From the experiences I have had with the djinn, I have become aware that the fear humans have for them has created an increasingly negative spiral. Djinn play out the negative aspects of human character. They play humans against each other, induce fear, and can drive people crazy. I feel that the reason they do this is both a mixture of their dislike for humans and their frustration about the world they live in, which is energetically dominated by human consciousness (which I have to admit is a good reason to be frustrated).

However, if you approach the djinn without fear and with respect and an open heart, they are not negative beings at all. It is possible to communicate with them and to make agreements with them. On a minimal level, we have begun to collaborate. They helped me with a subtle energy problem that I could not resolve because I did not know the beings involved. The djinn knew them, and they gave me the information that was needed to resolve the issue. This is an example of learning to work with subtle realms in a way that is mutually beneficial for all concerned.

IN-BETWEEN BEINGS

I returned to the topic of subtle beings who, according to the Sidhe, initially were able to move between our two worlds. I wanted to know more about these beings. I was also curious why the Sidhe allowed such a movement to happen.

We can read in your mind that you are aware of the kind of beings able to move between our worlds. Before going into more detail, we would like to share that some within the group of beings that were initially moving between our worlds were blocked access after a while. You know these beings as the gargoyles.

Over time, they picked up more of the lower vibrations of your world and were no longer welcome. There are beings, however, who still move between our worlds and some who have chosen to stay in our world. There is a group of beings who chose to be in our world because they cannot survive in your world for longer periods of time, but they are in complete harmony in our world. However, they can visit people in your world and sometimes even communicate with them. You know them as the unicorns.

When we talk about bridging the two worlds, the unicorns can be of great help. They have never been influenced by the energies of your world. They have always remained in the beauty of their essence as true gems in the world of Gaia. Their role, as we now understand it, has always been to be independent of the choices that you or we were making. They are always available to support all developments that support Gaia as a whole.

The unicorns are in direct communication with Gaia in a way that is also beyond the understanding of the Sidhe. However, we greatly honor their presence and support them in every way we can. We never have understood their choice to stay in contact with the human race. As we now see, they have never given up on you and the path you had chosen.

While we share this with you, we see that you also have a personal

connection with them. You are even aware that there are several species of unicorns. As we said, we do not understand the function they
have or the role of the different species. We perceive their energies
as always having variations of gentle power and unconditional love.
They are loved by all animals and plants in our world.

We received your unspoken question about the number of uni-
corn species. We are aware that you know three species. We know
of five different species of unicorns. The two species that you have
not yet met rarely travel between our worlds, if at all. The one that
you perceive as being the size of an elk with rainbow skin is the one
that visits your world most often. It is because of the size that your
consciousness has given unicorns the shape of horses, which as you
know is incorrect.

I was very happy with the Sidhe's willingness to share about unicorns. I
know that the majority of people believe that unicorns are part of fairy tales.
In all honesty, until a couple of years ago, I did too. One day we did a meditation with unicorns at our weekly crystal skull gathering.[3] That is the first time
I met the three species. That moment of connection has deeply touched me.
Their energies are difficult to describe; however, one word gives some indication: "purity."

I am now aware that they can truly help to bridge the worlds of Gaia. It
feels to me that in their own unique way, that is what they are already doing.
By reconnecting and collaborating with them, we might be able to speed up
the bridging of the different subtle worlds, especially between the world of
the Sidhe and ours.

The Sidhe mentioned that I knew that the shape of the horse for the unicorns was incorrect. This emanated from the first moment I saw them. They
appeared to me more like a variation of deer than horses. They also have two
toes instead of one, as horses have, which makes them more similar to deer
than horses.

Due to the way we had been sharing, I was aware when information
about a certain subject had come to an end. Although I would have liked to
hear more about unicorns, I knew that this would not happen in this phase
of our sharing. There was still one more group that I wanted to discuss. They

read my mind, and I felt the Sidhe readying to discuss them. They are also mythical beings — beings of legends and innumerable stories — and nowadays even movies: the dragons.

DRAGONS

Dragons are beings with which I have a deep connection. Jeanne and I have given several workshops about dragons, and I continue to study them. Therefore, I am incredibly curious about what the Sidhe would share.

We can telepathically receive considerable information from you because of your connection with them and because you work so intensely with them. Without any hesitation, we can say that we see dragons as another way to bring our worlds together. There are, however, considerable differences between the energies from the dragons with which we connect and the energies of those with which you connect.

There are dragons that exist in both worlds. These are the ones that can help to bridge our worlds. Because we are not completely sure whether we read your mind correctly, we would like to share what we perceive to see whether or not we are correct.

We see that you separate the dragons into three groups. The numbers in each group are based on the number four, which is the number of the four elements. It is also the number that is associated with Earth.

The first group consists of four dragons, which is one times four (one group of four). These dragons are what you call the ancient dragons, masters of the earth's basic energies that underlie all aspects of Earth. The second group has eight dragons, which is two times four (two groups of four). Two is the number of duality, which is a reflection of the way humans function in their physical world. You see this as a way to master human reality so as to transcend it. The third group consists of twelve dragons, which is three times four (three groups of four). Three is the number of oneness. These are the dragons that you believe will help humankind to move to a world that is based on oneness in which all is connected.

We can see that originally you had perceived three different dragons as the central dragon. You still believe that this is true but that there is also a dragon that functions as an overseer of all, and that dragon can also function as the central dragon for each of the three groups. Have we read your mind correctly?

Yes, they had, and they had done it in a surprisingly precise way.

Thank you. As you see, we are also learning. By now, you might be able to understand which dragons can be found in both our worlds. These are the dragons of the group of twelve plus the dragon that you call the master dragon. If there is one being that can help us, it is the master dragon. Of course, the group of twelve can also be of great help. They can truly help to bridge our worlds.

We know that you do not see dragons in the way they are depicted in your books and movies. You see the dragons as an aspect of the consciousness of Earth. They are a consciousness aspect of Gaia. They are flows — streams of energies — that you can pick up on and use for yourself to connect more deeply with the essence of who you are as it is supposed to be expressed within the Gaia consciousness.

These flows of energies and consciousness are entities that are completely independent. They can also take any form they want and do so as it seems fit to them. This may have created the basis for many of your stories. Because they are of energy, it might be human consciousness that created the forms.

We know that you call a person who has mastered the energies of one of the dragons a dragon rider and the one who masters the master dragon a dragon master. We understand very well what you mean. We have learned to flow (ride) with the energies of the thirteen dragons with which we connect. In your terminology, we are dragon riders.

Within our world, we do not have a dragon master. We now realize, thanks to your information, that we will never be able to become dragon masters. To become a dragon master, you also need to be connected to the physical aspects of Gaia. Because we have disconnected ourselves from the physical to the degree we have, we can never become dragon masters. We now realize that only human beings can reach the stage of being a true dragon master. Maybe those humans who reach that stage can become the true bridge between our worlds.

This sharing moved me into an unexpected direction. When I connected with dragons years ago, I knew that it was important to work with them. I have felt guided to work with them intensely over the last several years in order to develop ways to help people to connect to their essences and to the roles they have to fulfill in this world. However, I never expected that the connection with the Sidhe and their sharing would help me to see an even larger picture. I felt a deep gratitude for the guidance Gaia has given me that has brought me into contact with the Sidhe.

CHAPTER 12

QUESTIONS AND ANSWERS

I felt that we were reaching a point at which we had covered the major subjects the Sidhe wanted to share. I had no idea how we would proceed after this sharing, but I trusted that things would unfold exactly as they were supposed to unfold as viewed from the larger perspective. My feeling was that the one essence who had this larger perspective would be Gaia.

While I felt that soon we needed to end this period of intense contact, I desired to create an opportunity to ask them a few more questions. I also felt that some kind of conclusion was needed about what we had achieved. Also, there was the important question of how the representatives of the Sidhe and humans would be able to continue the process of cocreating the new consciousness.

The Sidhe agreed to be available to address additional subjects, and the final chapters would complete this phase of our interaction. In this chapter, I summarize my questions and the responses the Sidhe gave.

There was also a personal reason for agreeing to a break in our interactions. The period of interaction was both extremely intense and time-consuming for me. I felt that I was coming close to the maximum of what my system could handle. I needed time to recover, integrate, and process.

HISTORY

My first question had to do with the history of our two races. Both races had gone through different phases. I wished to know more about these phases and whether there were periods in which the Sidhe and humans had more contact. Moreover, I wondered whether the story of Adam and Eve, who had to leave paradise, had something to do with the separation of our two races.

Your questions bring us to our definition of what history really is. The way the Sidhe look at history is that it is a consciousness stream within the population of Sidhe in a certain moment. When there are changes in a population, its history will also change. In other words, we do not believe that history is constant or fixed. It is the point of view of the collective consciousness of a species or of the group or groups within a species.

Within the consciousness of a species, certain events are exceptionally important and thus remain in the history of the species. The details change over time, and the main events come back in whatever form people give them in that moment. We are highly aware of this.

In comparison to yours, the Sidhe have had a world that has been very stable. Nonetheless, there have been many changes over long periods in the way we see our world. We are aware of this and accept it as something that is inevitable. Therefore, we do not have any need to argue about our history with each other.

We know that individual communities in different parts of our world will see details in various ways. Therefore, the Sidhe do not believe in a "right" history. We only believe in a perception of history that reflects our consciousness in the most optimal way in any given moment. The major constants in our history are the separation and the development to create a world that could protect the Sidhe heritage in the most advantageous way.

From our perspective, we believe that this is also true for humans, even though you might disagree. The difference, however, is that there have been numerous changes within the human world. In the course of your history, humans were not able to communicate telepathically. Therefore, it was impossible to create a history that covered the whole human species. For that reason, there are different stories in different parts of your world. Examples are the great civilizations your history describes that never covered the whole world. Only in recent times, with the modern technological means of communication, is it possible to spread information over the whole world, at least to a large degree.

There is another phenomenon in your world that is worthy of consideration: the phenomenon of manipulation of information. Humans are able to purposely spread false information to mislead the majority of the population. This has happened throughout your history and is still happening today. Due to the current communication technology, it has become even easier to spread false information. This indicates that history by definition is to a large degree manipulated and incorrect. We felt that it was important to share this first, because all that we will be sharing has to be seen in the light of what we just said.

Let us start with your story of Adam and Eve. We find this an interesting story that, in our opinion, has two aspects. One aspect is the part of being kicked out of paradise. The other is the idea that two human beings formed the basis of the whole of humankind.

We believe the story that Adam and Eve had to leave paradise because they had eaten from the tree of knowledge is a slight twist on the story of separation. It was not so much the tree of knowledge with which they were connecting. The actual eating of a physical fruit was a symbol of moving deeper into physicality; therefore, those who became the Sidhe disconnected from them, and the humans lost paradise. Humans might feel that they were sent out of paradise. The reality is, however, that they lost it.

We believe the story of a man and a woman that started the human race is an interesting reflection of the different phases that humankind has gone through during their history. We believe human beings have continually tried to create their own version of paradise. It is an aspect of a consciousness stream that will always be present, whether conscious or subconscious.

Repeatedly, humans have created civilizations that had many aspects of paradise. However, these civilizations were always eventually destroyed. This is also a reflection of the separation that repeats itself many times in your world, because it is an inherent aspect of your consciousness stream. The man and woman who start the world is a story that is so abundantly present in your world that it can be seen as a symbol for each beginning of a new world. It is the start of what could be a new world that could bring back the paradise that you subconsciously long for.

You also asked about the periods in which you reached a higher level of spiritual development and whether the Sidhe had contact with humans during these periods. As we mentioned before, there have been connections between Sidhe and humans throughout history. This has never happened on a large scale, and the interactions were not just during the periods of what you call your highly developed ancient civilizations.

Human beings have always been physically oriented, even in periods of high development; therefore, there never was a longing from the Sidhe for a deeper connection. However, we have been connecting with humans throughout time.

After the separation, the most extensive connection between our two races was during what you call your Lemuria period. In those times, many humans understood the connection with nature spirits. The connections of humans with plants and animals was also still very deep in that period. It was then that humankind came closest to the Sidhe. As a consequence, there was comparatively much more contact and sharing.

That was a period in which representatives of the human race visited our world. This was always done with care and only in certain areas under certain circumstances. In those days, the connections were always satisfactory for both sides. As you know, this did not last. These experiences have made us very cautious about connecting with any member of your race.

Another group that we have had contact with are those you call your medicine people and shamans. These contacts never led them to visit us, but we visited them to help them in certain areas, often by their request. However, these contacts have almost completely disappeared and are no longer desired by the Sidhe. Now we are in a phase of renewed connection brought about through necessity.

I thanked the Sidhe very much. Their sharing was most helpful. I noticed that they mentioned only Lemuria and not Atlantis, and I wondered whether that meant they had less contact with the people in the Atlantis period.

That is correct. There were people from Lemuria who went to Atlantis and later became the ones you call the indigenous people of that area?. The overall energy of Atlantis had far less resonance with the Sidhe world than the energies Lemuria did. Atlantis was the beginning of what we call the great destruction phase that led to the situation that we are facing now, from both the Sidhe and the human perspectives. This brings us to another point we have not yet talked about: technology.

The Sidhe do not have technology. We do not need it. Gaia as a whole has been created in such a way that if you know how to use what is offered, you can create all that you need through intent and with the collaboration of nature spirits. For us, this is so clear and obvious that we do not understand why humans cannot comprehend it. To some degree, you did this during the time of Lemuria, but that was lost and replaced by technology in Atlantis.

Because of the energies and the flow of consciousness in Atlantis, the descendants of Lemuria also lost many of their skills. After the destruction of Atlantis, even more skills that were related to working with nature and nature spirits were lost. The attempt to re-create the technological approach of Atlantis in your current times has led to a technology that can destroy this planet within seconds.

Another aspect of technology is your tendency to place the power that you personally have into your instruments, and consequently, you disempower yourself and tend to no longer develop your skills. Why would you? Why make effort to learn to communicate telepathically when you can take one of your gadgets and call somebody at the other end of the world. However, the consequences are dire. This is hardly recognized by the majority of humans. We know that some of you are aware. Generally, current technology has caused you to become further spiritually disconnected from yourselves and others.

You are also very aware that the development of your technology has only contributed to further breakdown of your world. We know that you are aware that consciousness can change anything. In theory, you can, as a species, change the world that you live in. This depends on your vibrational state, your clarity of consciousness, and your ability to work with nature spirits and beings from the subtle worlds. We put it this way because we are more or less expressing what your mind is already thinking.

We are also aware that even though you believe this, you can seem quite desperate when you observe the unwillingness of the majority of humans to change. You already mentioned that people have the idea that they will lose something if they have to change. Because we do not have technology, many humans will see us as primitive and would never want to give up their toys, even though they are frustrated with the world they live in.

What the Sidhe shared is a sad truth. In all honesty, if I were a Sidhe, I would not want to connect with the human race as a whole. However, I also love people, and I love the world I live in. I am willing to do anything that I can to contribute to a process of change and transformation. For me, it is simple: As long as Gaia has not yet given up on us, there is still time. Let us use the time that she gives us wisely and help each other as much as we can.

CONNECTION

There was another subject that I knew many humans who want to contribute to the creation of a new consciousness might ask: How can we connect with the Sidhe? I immediately felt that this was "one of those questions." I could feel that they still did not like the idea of connecting with humans. I was curious what they would say about this.

Once we are in telepathic communication, we cannot hide much from you, especially because our connection has become much stronger. We are actually shocked that you understand what really happens with so much of what is called Sidhe contact.

[Note: Here the Sidhe are referring to something that I became aware of during our telepathic connection. They thought that they had hidden it from me because this information was not in the vibrational stream of our standard communication. I could feel that they would prefer that I not share this information. I have no idea why I was able to receive it.]

At this time, we rely on you to feel what can be shared about this subject to guarantee the continuation of collaboration with those who want to work with us. There are many things we can say and you can say. We ask that when you share about us to respect our privacy and acknowledge the importance of a plan to create a new consciousness, identifying the ways that we can work with each other.

As you know, the use of the morphogenetic grid as a way to connect remains difficult for us. Therefore, we would appreciate it if you would no longer use that method. We have already taken some measurements, but more is needed to not disrupt our society.

For me, the most important aspect of our sharing and connection was to totally honor the Sidhe's request about not making contact through the morphogenetic grid. Some of the people from the group who were present when we used the morphogenetic grid as a way to contact them became aware of that request, and I know they will honor it. I also wanted to telepathically share a way for the Sidhe to further protect themselves from unexpected use of the morphogenetic grid, which I will not reveal here.

CONNECTION WITH THE SUN

Another subject that was mentioned in the beginning of our sharing was the connection of the Sidhe with the Sun. There was no other reference to this subject, but I felt that it was important to ask the Sidhe to share more about their relationship with the Sun.

We are glad that you bring up this subject, because it is indeed an important one. While we stay connected as much as we can with the star systems with which we resonate to maintain the connection with our essences, we are also very aware that we are part of Gaia and of the star that gives life to all that lives on her. We are also aware of the other planets and their effects on us.

From our perspective, the Sun is the key to life on Earth and therefore also our lives. We cannot live without the Sun. While most people are aware that the Sun is a life giver, they are not aware of other important aspects of the Sun.

The Sun is the gateway for receiving all of the information for our solar system. The Sun gathers information from the universe and transforms it in such a way as to support all life on all planets in the whole solar system. You talk only about the planets that are physical, which means the ones that are visible for you. However, there are also planets connected to the Sun that you do not see, because they do not have the vibrational frequencies that you can perceive. Of course, the phenomenon of invisible planets and even invisible stars is common throughout the universe.

While each planet radiates energies that affect you as is described in your astrology, so also will the invisible planets. However, their influence will mainly be on your etheric and astral systems. Because we too are not physical, they have a more direct influence on us than on you. As far as we know, there are three of these planets. Maybe we should say this differently: We are able to perceive three planets that are invisible to you in our solar system. We do not want to talk about these planets, but we mention them to allow you to envision the solar system from a larger perspective and to expand your view of the subtle worlds beyond Gaia. But let us go back to the Sun.

In your way of thinking, we need to be protected from certain aspects of the Sun. This is true. What most people are not aware of is that the Sun also forms a certain shield around the solar system. That shield protects us from some of the radiation from the universe. However, the most important aspect of the Sun is that it collects information. As you know, all energies contain information. The shield of the Sun collects energy and translates it into information that is suitable for this solar system. Each shield around a planet does the same thing.

In other words, Gaia receives the information from the Sun and transforms it into information suitable for her system. At the same time, she allows those frequencies and information to come through that can be received and worked with directly by those living within Gaia's system.

In our world, the connection with the Sun is critically important. It also has been important in many civilizations and traditions in your world. Learning to connect with the consciousness of the Sun will help you to raise your vibration and will allow you direct access to information you might want to use for the expansion of your consciousness. The Sun provides all that you need, but you have to open yourself up to these gifts. Of course, we do not only talk about physical gifts but also spiritual gifts. Whatever a species needs is available.

People believe that they can live on the energy of the Sun only. We believe that the Sun provides all that we need but that some of what the Sun makes available needs to be transformed by Gaia. Therefore, we believe that we need the energies of both the Sun and from Gaia.

Although all that we need is provided by the Sun and by Gaia, we need to ask for it to receive it. Both humans and Sidhe live in realities in which free will is an important paradigm that is respected by all higher consciousness. For that reason, we have to ask Gaia and the Sun for what we want from them. The Sidhe always believed that they asked the right questions because they always got the support of the Sun for all that was needed to maintain, what you call, our paradise.

However, we are now aware of the fact that we might have asked only a part of the questions we were supposed to ask because we did not include the whole. We would like to suggest to you that it is time for human beings to reconnect with the essence of the Sun. Maybe you would do better by asking the right questions that could lead to a shift in your and Gaia's energy and, as a consequence, within the whole energy of the solar system.

We get energies from Earth for the well-being of our etheric and astral systems, and we receive energies from the Sun for the well-being of our total system. This is also true for you, even though the energies themselves might be different.

THE DIVINE SPARK

The last subject I wanted to touch on was the definition of a soul. My Sidhe friends had already mentioned a few things, but it was important to have the information summarized clearly, so I asked for their definition of a soul.

We are aware that human beings use the term "soul" lightly. We are also aware that different people use the term in different ways. We are willing to give a description of our way of looking at the human/ Sidhe system that might help you. We know that similar ideas exist in your world.

We see both our being and your being as consisting of three major parts. The first part is the physical system. In your case, this includes three parts: physical, etheric, and astral. In our case, this includes two parts: etheric and astral. The second part is the higher self, which you define as also consisting of three bodies: the emotional, the mental (or causal), and the spiritual. The third part is the soul.

The soul is a divine spark, a divine essence that is a unit that can work independently from other spiritual sparks (souls). At the same time, all souls are totally interconnected with other souls and form groups, which you call soul groups. We do not remember what defines the formation of soul groups, but their function is to support each member of that group, especially the members of the group that are incarnated.

The soul decides to incarnate and connect with a physical body (in the case of your world, Earth). In this connection, a third aspect is formed, which you call a higher self. This higher self is actually the bridge between the physical and the soul, forming a kind of buffer between these two.

The vibrational difference between the physical body and the soul is challenging to live with for most humans. The quality of the high self is determined by both the physical system and the soul and reflects the way these two parts communicate. It also reflects the quality of how well the physical system functions.

After the physical system dies, the high self stays connected to the soul. The soul stays earthbound until the moment it can express through the high self and the physical system what it came here to do. This is the basis of reincarnation, the cycle of birth, death, and rebirth in the search for ways to allow the soul to express itself in this world. When that happens, the high self is in total harmony with the soul. The Sidhe are as much caught in this cycle as humans are. That is one of the main reasons why we believe that we need to collaborate in whatever way works for all concerned. We hope that you understand our definitions now.

I thanked Sha and Ki very much. I understood their definitions, and I strongly resonated with them. I am sure that many people will understand these definitions. However, understanding is different from living it as a way to escape from the prison of the collective. Escaping from the prison of the collective might also be the way to escape from the cycles of reincarnation because we finally do what we said we came here to do.

I felt that we had reached an end to the direct communications of phase one. I set the intent that there would be a follow-up, especially with more practical applications and information to truly move toward a new consciousness. The final chapter will summarize a number of things from the sharing and will offer practical suggestions about how people can train themselves to be able to move toward this new consciousness.

CHAPTER 13

THE BIRTH OF A NEW CONSCIOUSNESS

We have arrived at the final chapter of my unexpected journey. It was an intense — often almost too intense — but immensely rewarding experience. While my journey seemed to be characterized by dialogues with the Sidhe, this was not its main purpose. Finding ways to get out of our self-induced consciousness prison was the goal. The true purpose of this spiritual journey was about reconnecting with a consciousness that reflects our true essence. We learned that we are not alone on such a path. The Sidhe did not only invite us to go on our own spiritual explorations, but they also invited us to support each other on our respective journeys. This realization makes it crystal clear that our sharing had a purpose beyond simply connecting with the Sidhe.

Many times during this odyssey, I felt an invitation to break through the limitations of our collective consciousness. We really live in a matrix with cords that binds us. We continually tell ourselves and others that we are free and have free choices, but the reality differs. We are locked within a world filled with limitations that are based on beliefs we share and keep alive. All of the promises from teachers and systems rarely lead to freedom.

Why did I so often hear the invitation to break free? I am sure many of you have felt the same. So why do we still feel locked within the matrix? The reason is obvious: We have not yet found a way out. The only escape is to connect to the morphogenetic field that we share with the Sidhe. Initially, I thought that this would be easy. Although it is just a matter of refocusing from the morphogenetic grid to the field, it turns out not to be simple at all. Interestingly, this challenge is the same for the Sidhe. Because both of us are looking for ways to get out of our respective matrixes (morphogenetic grids) and reconnect with the same morphogenetic field, we may be able to help each other. Still, based on these sharings, it is clear there remains an enormous gap between us.

Whether we choose to work with the Sidhe or not, there is one thing that we need to do. We need to raise our vibration. Raising our vibration means that we need to transform all our energies, emotions, and thoughts that are of a lower vibration, for example, fear-based thoughts and emotions. This is primary because the connection with the Sidhe in this stage of human consciousness is not likely to happen for most people. Even when there is a connection with the Sidhe, it does not help someone to escape the prison of the grid. We need to start doing some major inner work first. Yes, suggestions from the Sidhe are helpful. It will also be helpful to check regularly with them to see where, from their perspective, we are with respect to our efforts in raising our vibrations.

The Sidhe and humans share the aspiration to break free of their respective matrices, their respective morphogenetic grids. However, their paths to accomplish this will be notably different. The path that human beings need to take is in many ways more challenging than that of the Sidhe because the human matrix keeps humans locked in a physical world. Humans are caught up in their daily survival and spend most of their time earning money to be able to eat, clothe themselves, and have a roof over their heads. For most people, this requires so much energy that the idea of raising their vibration is merely a sweet dream. At best, it is something they are able to do to limited degrees for short periods of time. Many people mainly experience a heavy, vibrationally dense, and tiring perspective of our world. In their experience, it seems impossible to escape survival mode.

Now is the time for us to make different choices. We can continue to look at the world as heavy and difficult, and assuredly, nothing will change. We cannot change if we choose to think about the world in the same way we have been conditioned and have gotten used to living. Einstein is often credited with saying, "We cannot solve our problems with the same level of thinking that created them." Regardless of the source, the message is valid. We need to learn to think differently. Talking to the Sidhe, working with other beings, and being willing to look at the world differently will open doors that many believe do not exist. However, we need to do the actual work of change, primarily from the point of the physical aspects.

We are spiritual beings, although many people have forgotten this. Our challenge is not to be spiritual but to be physical. We have chosen to come to Earth to experience physical reality for whatever reasons we decided before incarnation. Now that we are here, we need to learn to live optimally in this physical world. We can only transcend the matrix of the physical reality when we deeply know and master it. Raising our vibrations and expanding our consciousnesses offer us the possibilities to increasingly master our physical realities, thereby allowing us to bring more aspects of our spiritual essence into this world and helping to raise the vibration of Gaia as a whole. And this will help to bridge the distance between the Sidhe and humans that might help both of us to reconnect to the morphogenetic field.

In this chapter, I will summarize a couple of methods that can help you raise your vibrations, connect more with the Sidhe, and begin to reconnect with the morphogenetic field. I will offer some basic exercises and meditations, but recognize that there are more tools available. Extensive tools are beyond the scope of this book and might be offered in the future in other, more appropriate formats. If you were to work diligently with what is offered here, your vibration will undoubtedly increase.

STEPPING OUT OF FEAR

The most important step in raising your vibration is to diminish the amount of fear in your life and, ultimately, to live fearlessly. In the movie *After Earth*,[1] Will Smith, playing the character Cypher, formulated it perfectly: "Danger is very real, but fear is a choice." This is absolutely true. Fear is a chosen scenario that arises from a situation that is dangerous or seems that way. Danger increases the production of adrenaline to deal with the situation at hand. Fear, however, induces stress hormones that make us ineffective or even dysfunctional.

If we want to raise our vibration, we need to prevent fear from controlling our state of being. When we find ourselves in a state of fear, we need to have a way to release fear. Learning to release fear is important because most people regularly experience fear in different forms, inducing seemingly challenging, difficult, and emotional situations that are not real but imagined. These fears keep us locked in the matrix, the morphogenetic grids of our awareness, of our active consciousness. It is also our collective consciousness that induces fears. This is how we create the vicious circle of fear in our lives.

Jeanne and I give a full day's workshop to help people to develop tools to release fear. I cannot provide the whole workshop in this book; however, I am planning to include this information in a future book.[2] Because I consider the release of fear to be a key support on the path of birthing a new consciousness, I will summarize the essential points here. This information will help you do the exercise to release fear. You can train yourself to make this an integral part of your functioning. The guided training from our workshop makes it much easier for you to incorporate the system of releasing fear in your daily life. However, learning and practicing on your own is better than not having ways to release fear.

Fear has numerous faces and has been engrained into our systems in countless ways. Fear is reflected in our beliefs, emotions, and the collective consciousness grids. It is locked in our energy bodies, organs, and cells, and it is an inherent part of our minds. This means that stepping out of fear is a process that requires time, diligence, perseverance, willingness, and a clear intent to never give up, even though the process might at times be incredibly frustrating. We will never step into a new consciousness if we are not willing to undertake this path. And we will never make a real connection with the Sidhe.

The process of stepping out of fear has three major steps: connecting with your heart (divine essence), connecting with the frontal lobes of your brain, and the stimulation of the frontal part of your amygdalae. We will go through these three steps and then integrate them in a visualization to overcome and transform fear. The first part was mentioned in chapter 5, but with some modification, I will present it here again to give you the complete process.

Step 1: Connect with Your Heart
- *Close your eyes, and make yourself as comfortable as possible*
- *Take a few deep breaths, and allow yourself to relax. Focus on your breathing.*
- *Feel yourself relax more deeply.*
- *Now bring your awareness to the center of your heart. This is the location of*

your divine essence. You can imagine this essence as a sphere of white light. Allow this white light to shine throughout your whole physical system. Let it shine into every corner, into every cell.

- *Feel how this white light holds unconditional love that now has spread throughout your physical system. Guide this love to yourself. Feel unconditional love for yourself exactly as you are now.*
- *Sit in this energy for a while to allow your system to absorb it and become familiar with it.*
- *Take a deep breath, and open your eyes.*

Doing this meditation frequently will help you to increasingly connect with your divine essence, an integrated part of you, and will raise your vibration.

Step 2: Connect with Your Frontal Lobes

The frontal lobes, the frontal one-third of your brain, are fundamentally important, because this is the part of the brain that makes us truly human. It is the place of all of our higher faculties and is essential for stepping out of fear and increasing your vibration. In humans, the prefrontal cortex takes up the majority of the frontal lobes.

The prefrontal cortex is crucial for the performance of almost all of our skills requiring intelligence. It is the center of logically connecting things with each other. It is also the center of happiness, higher consciousness and awareness, and intuition. This is the part of the brain from which we desire to function and live our lives, as when we step out of fear. Otherwise, we will function mainly from the reptilian part of our brains, which is the part of the brain that functions when we are in a fear state.

- *Take a few deep inhalations and exhalations, and feel yourself relaxing. Allow your brain to relax, and feel yourself sinking into a deeper relaxation, going into a meditative state.*
- *By bringing your awareness to your breathing, you will relax even more. Simply breathe in a relaxed way.*
- *Now become aware of your brain as a whole. Can you feel whether it is active? Can you feel a particular part? Do not judge yourself if you cannot feel anything. We are not used to connecting with our brains. We are simply observing.*

- *Now move your awareness to the frontal one-third of your brain. Make a connection as deeply as possible and again feel that part to the best of your ability. Observe whether you can be aware of its energy, its activity. Simply explore it as well as you can and without judgment.*
- *Sit for a while in the energy of connecting with and exploring your frontal lobes.*
- *Again, take a deep breath. Bring your awareness back to where you are, and when you feel ready, open your eyes.*

Step 3: Stimulating the Frontal Part of Your Amygdalae

The third step requires explanation. It is called the amygdala switch. The amygdala is a key structure determining how we function in this world: whether we live in happiness and joy or in fear, worries, and frustration. We have excessively trained the amygdalae to be in a state that leads to unpleasant experiences, like worries, fear, frustration, anger, and many other fear-based emotions. In all of these unpleasant fear states, the back part of the amygdala is active. It is time to change this pattern and train a new habit, to activate the joy and happiness state of the amygdala. This stimulation is called "tickling the amygdala" because it must be done gently. In order to be effective, we need to have a general idea of the amygdala's location. It is not critical to locate its position with absolute precision. We only need to know its general position so that we can visualize it.

We have two amygdalae, one on each side (in each hemisphere) of the brain. To locate these amygdalae, each roughly the size and shape of an almond (hence its Greek name amygdala, which means almond), place your thumb in your ear and the middle finger at the outside edge of your eye socket where the bone makes a V-shape. Now let your index finger fall to the middle between your two fingers. You now have located the place from where you move one inch inside your head. Doing so, you find the location of the amygdalae at both sides of your brain.

Remember, to stimulate your amygdalae to be active in the frontal position, you need to touch it gently. Obviously, you cannot enter your brain, so you need to visualize. Because we need to do it gently, it is best to visualize stimulating the frontal part by tickling it with an imaginary feather. In your imagination, gently stroke the frontal part of your amygdalae at the same time.

Of course, you can stimulate the frontal part of your amygdalae in any way you prefer, as long as you do it gently. The feather is simply a symbol of gentleness.

Following are some more examples of ways to stimulate the frontal part of your amygdala:

- *Imagine gently stroking the frontal part of the amygdala with your fingers.*
- *Imagine activating the frontal part of your amygdala through intent alone.*
- *Imagine an energetic link between the frontal part of the amygdala and the frontal lobes.*

Try each of these methods to determine whether you feel any differences among them. Choose the one that works best for you to stimulate and activate the frontal part of your amygdala. You might think it is appropriate to use different methods at different times; however, I do not recommend such variation. Let your brain become familiar with the best method for you so that it becomes a habit, a pattern. Your most important tool is clear intention. The visualization is meant to support the power of intention. Ultimately, you will use only intention. However, do not drop the tools too quickly.

You will achieve an optimal effect when you integrate the three steps into one. In the beginning, it is preferable to do the steps separately, but once you can easily make each connection, you will be able to do all three steps in one meditative visualization flow: heart, frontal lobes, frontal part of the amygdala. Jeanne does this on her in-breath: heart, frontal lobes, tickling the amygdalae. Play with this so that you find the best form for you.

If you cannot feel a connection after setting the intent to connect, do not worry. The intent is enough. Just trust that it works, and then move on. Here is a meditation integrating all three steps.

Stepping Out of Fear: All Three Steps in One Flow

- *Close your eyes, and take a few full inhalations and exhalations.*
- *Bring your awareness to your heart, and to the best of your ability, connect with the divine essence within. Let the light of your divine essence shine throughout your whole system, and feel yourself pulsating with love for yourself.*
- *While you stay connected with your heart and with unconditional love, bring your awareness to the frontal one-third of your brain, the frontal lobes. To the best of your ability, feel that you have made that connection.*

- *Be fully aware of your connection with both your heart and your frontal lobes, and feel love and gratitude for all that the frontal lobes do for you.*
- *Now imagine that while you are sending unconditional love as you are connected with both your heart and your frontal lobes, you are tickling the frontal part of your amygdalae in the way that works best for you.*
- *To the best of your ability, observe and feel what happens.*
- *Do not get frustrated if you do not seem to feel all the connections at the same time. When you set the intent, the connections will be made whether you feel them or not.*
- *After the tickling, stay in these connections and energies for as long as feels comfortable.*
- *When you feel ready, express your gratitude, take a deep breath, and open your eyes again.*

You can do this with your eyes closed or open, anytime, anywhere, to eliminate any fear. The more you train, the easier you can shift. This could be one of the most important visualizations you will ever learn. This visualization can change your life, bring you to a state of bliss, and awaken your total system. It is the foundation for the shift into a new consciousness. It is also the key to stepping out — unplugging — from the morphogenetic grids, our collective consciousness, that holds us in its grip.

Whenever you want to set intent, whenever you would like to use any other way to move into a new consciousness based on the morphogenetic field, always start with this visualization. I consistently practice this, and it has helped me tremendously in my life.

USING CRYSTAL SKULLS

I have written two books on crystal skulls[3]; therefore, I will not go into details here. The main thing that crystal skulls have taught me is that they help us in our growth in so many ways that I now consider them to be my favorite support to raise my vibrations. I believe that they are able to help us connect with the morphogenetic field and help us to unplug from the morphogenetic grid.

There is, however, one challenge with crystal skulls. They have many qualities, one of which is that they are amplifiers. They amplify every kind of energy. That is the reason that it is important to use them in such a way that they stimulate and amplify the energies that will help us to raise our vibrations to allow us to reconnect with our true essences. This true essence can be found in the morphogenetic field but not in the grids.

To use the crystal skulls in the best way, it is recommended that you use the Stepping Out of Fear visualization first. It also brings you into a connection with your divine essence that will guide you to use the crystal skulls in the most optimal way. Even after studying crystal skulls for more than twenty years, I still do not know everything that they can offer us. What I do know is that they have the potential to help us shift into a consciousness that helps to fulfill the agreement we made with Gaia: to raise the vibration of Earth and all that lives on it to such a degree that ascension will be possible. For those who would like to use this way of expansion, I refer you to the aforementioned books.

WORKING WITH NATURE SPIRITS

Fear has caused us to disconnect and feel separated from most everything that exists in our world. It has disconnected us from the subtle realms even more. And because we cannot observe these realms with our normal five senses, we hardly know that they exist. Because it is difficult to be aware of what happens in the invisible subtle realms, fear is easily induced. Many human beings are afraid of what they cannot control, such as nature spirits.

There are two major reasons to relearn how to work with nature spirits:

- They can help us to understand more about the world in which we live. This makes it possible to reconnect with Gaia and all that exists within her system that enables us to become stewards of this system.
- Connecting with nature spirits can help us to connect with the Sidhe. As we have heard, there is a strong connection between the Sidhe and nature spirits. Therefore, the nature spirits can act as intermediaries, assisting the Sidhe and us in our connection.

Additionally, in order to connect and work with the nature spirits, we have to make changes within ourselves that also make it easier for us to connect with the Sidhe. Even if we do not choose to connect with the Sidhe, nature spirits help us to understand the world in which we live, and we can again become conscious cocreators with them.

The worlds of nature spirits are vast. We begin with an entrance into their worlds and then allow this connection to grow organically, in a natural way. When you enter a subtle world, you need to prepare yourself. That is why I started with training in stepping out of fear. You have to start by diminishing your fears because nature spirits can be sensitive. They do not like human fear energies because they disrupt the world of nature.

Connecting with nature spirits is easiest and best done in nature; however, you can connect with them inside your home. There are nature spirits everywhere, and they are connected with stones, plants, trees, and animals. They are also connected with water, forests, mountains, and the like. Each individual can explore the kind of nature spirit with whom he or she has the strongest resonance.

To connect with nature spirits (after you have removed yourself as much as you can from the fear state) find a quiet, comfortable place. Once you have settled yourself, connect with your divine essence, and then set the intention to open yourself to connect with a nature spirit who can help you on your journey of fulfilling your purpose. Then you enter into the most challenging phase: relax, wait, and see. Feel whether you can perceive something.

When you feel the presence of a nature spirit, first honor and acknowledge its presence. Ask the nature spirit to increase the strength of its energies to make the connection stronger and easier for you. Never judge your experience, and always trust that you have made a step forward, whether you have perceived something or not. Do this regularly, and without exception, you will make an increasingly deep connection with the world of nature spirits. To learn more about connecting with nature spirits, I highly recommend the stimulating work of David Spangler.[4]

CONNECTING WITH THE UNICORNS

From sharing with the Sidhe, I learned that unicorns can be helpful in bridging the worlds between the humans and the Sidhe — as well as the human world with other subtle worlds. Moreover, they can help us grow into the new consciousness that is connected with the morphogenetic field.

The best way to connect with unicorns is to let go of all preconceived ideas about them. Become like a child exploring something new. Initially, a child is devoid of beliefs and therefore is still completely open. This is the attitude with which to approach the unicorns. Because these wonderful beings open themselves equal to the degree you are able to open to them, we can experience unicorns in numerous ways. My experience is not yours, and it is preferable that you create your own unique connection. That is part of their magic: The connection they establish is unique to you and helps you to see the magical being that you are.

There are countless different worlds within the Gaia system. These worlds might appear as separate in the consciousness of those who are looking at them. In reality, all worlds within Gaia are one. Unicorns help bridge the different consciousness systems to allow each consciousness to see the different worlds as one again, even though their vibrations might vary. They can help us bridge the worlds of the Sidhe and humans and thus contribute to the creation of a new consciousness.

As you read earlier in this book, the unicorns no longer live in our world (our vibrational reality), but they can hear your call when it is pure and comes from your heart, and they will come. To make your call as pure as possible, first do the exercise to step out of fear. Then return to your divine essence, and call them. It is important to be patient when you are trying to establish a connection with unicorns. It may not happen the first time or even the tenth time. That does not mean that there is something wrong with you. It just means that the right vibration is yet to happen. Most likely, they have heard your call, they came to you, and you were not able to perceive them.

The motto here is this: Never give up. The process will open your heart more, and rewards will come in whatever way is appropriate for you in that moment. In the meantime, you are definitely raising your vibration.

CONNECTING WITH DRAGONS

As was mentioned earlier, dragons have become an important part of my personal world and development. I plan to write a book based on all of the research and the workshops that Jeanne and I have given.[2,5] The subject is so vast that it is beyond the scope of this book. Therefore, I will share some suggestions about working with dragons that will help you get started and allow you to connect with them deeply enough to begin to explore their world on your own or with like-minded people. However, to learn to connect with all twenty-seven species and to learn about their gifts, proper guidance is needed, either from the dragons themselves or from a person who has extensively studied them.

As the Sidhe shared — and I totally agree with them — dragons are consciousness streams of Gaia. These streams of consciousness function as completely independent entities. They have no form but can take form and can induce images in your mind. These images are more of a reflection of the person than of the actual energies.

The dragon energies are meant to help us master the reality determined by the morphogenetic grids in such a way that we are no longer limited by it. To use our former terminology, they help us master the world of the morphogenetic grids in such a way that we can open ourselves to the morphogenetic field.

In chapter 11, it was mentioned that there are three groups of dragons totaling twenty-seven species. Their energies and their qualities help us understand the basic Earth energies, the energies we need to create our reality in a dualistic world and shift into living in oneness. As mentioned, this requires much study, and to understand their gifts, proper guidance is recommended.

There is a group of thirteen dragons that can help us to prepare for a new consciousness. They are also the ones that can help us to connect with the Sidhe on a deeper and more expanded level. That makes it possible for both the Sidhe and humans to increasingly support each other to move beyond our respective matrices.

To learn to recognize and optimally work with each of the dragon species is a long journey. Those who do want to travel this journey have to find their own way, wait for my forthcoming book on dragons, or follow our workshops.[5] It is most useful for you to connect with a dragon who can support you on your journey in the most optimal way in the moment. To call such a dragon, you do not need to know what kind of dragon answers your call. You need to trust that when you call a dragon, the right dragon will always come to help you in the most ideal way possible.

To ensure an optimal connection, I suggest that you first do the exercise to eliminate fear. When you are in fear, your encounter could be unpleasant, and you could attract beings other than dragons who might not be supportive. Next, you go to your divine essence, and from your divine essence, you call in the dragon that in this moment can best help you on your journey of expansion and evolution into the new consciousness. Then sit in the energies for as long as feels comfortable, allowing them to unfold.

CONNECTION WITH THE SIDHE

As we mentioned before, the goal of this book is not to work with the Sidhe. The goal is to raise your vibrations to be able to enter a new consciousness by connecting increasingly with the morphogenetic field. The goal is to disconnect from the confinements of the morphogenetic grids that hold us prisoner, as seen from a consciousness perspective. Several ways have been given to help you on your journey. The connection with the Sidhe seems to be the most important one. However, I do not believe that this is true.

It is not easy to establish a connection with the Sidhe, and my feeling is that they are the ones who choose with whom they want to connect. I hear about many people who claim to have a connection with the Sidhe. However, most of these connections are actually with nature spirits. From a certain perspective, it does not matter. But focusing too much on the connection with the Sidhe might actually prevent you from finding the best way to raise your vibration and to contribute to the new consciousness. This is also the reason that the Sidhe I have contacted (Sha and Ki and their community) did not give a specific exercise to connect with them. They said that enough has been said about raising your vibration, which could lead to a connection with them or not. It will definitely guide you to where you need to go to fulfill your purpose in life.

Sha and Ki would also like you to refer to other published methods that have been given by the Sidhe. One is the glyph that has been given to John Matthews in his Sidhe contact.[6] This is a symbol that can be used to establish contact. Another approach is to work with the card deck that has been produced by David Spangler and Jeremy Berg under the guidance of the Sidhe.[7] Whatever tool you use, always do so from a connection with your divine essence after having diminished fear as much as possible, which is far more important than the use of any tool.

CONCLUSION

The conclusion can be summarized in image 13.1. It shows that there is a relationship between Infinite Consciousness and Gaia and that they exchange

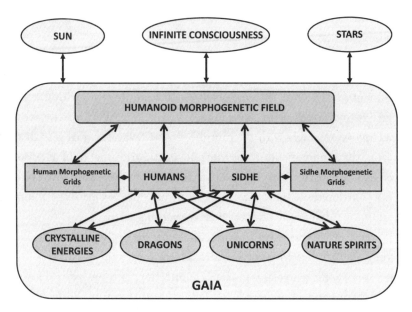

Image 13.1: Relationships with and within Gaia that support the process of creating a new consciousness (see text).

energy and information, making it a dynamic system. Within the Gaia system is a humanoid morphogenetic field that is part of the Gaia consciousness field. This humanoid morphogenetic field results in, among others, the human and the Sidhe morphogenetic grids. These grids determine the way humans and Sidhe look, function, and behave. There are four main systems that both humans and Sidhe connect with. These four systems can help bridge the gap between the Sidhe and humans.

The Sidhe helped us to realize the dire situation humankind is in, and they are willing to help us to evolve out of our collectively created consciousness prison. They realize that they are actually in a similar situation — although their prison is much more pleasant. Both races will stay in their prisons if they are unwilling to make the effort to find ways to evolve. This effort to evolve is a personal choice. For human beings, it is the path of doing everything you can to raise your vibration to such a level that the momentum is created that frees you from the human collective consciousness. Such freedom offers the possibility to connect with the field of your full potential; this field we call the morphogenetic field.

Once we are connected with the morphogenetic field, we will speed up the remembering of who we truly are. The connection with the morphogenetic field will also speed up the development of the many unused skills we possess. This process will help us to reconnect with Gaia as a whole, become an integrated part of it, and fulfill our purpose — namely the new consciousness, which is where the Sidhe would also like to arrive. Although their path is different from ours, we can support each other and collaborate in the future. After all, we have in common the realization that it is important to connect with the Sun and with the stars guided by Source, or the Infinite Consciousness.

There are many beings who are willing to help us. We would surely be wise to use all of the support available to us. We are the ones who have to make the choices. We have to be willing to do what it takes to achieve the state of new consciousness. We do not have to do it alone, but we have to do it ourselves. If you feel beckoned, I wish you a wonderful journey toward this new consciousness.

EPILOGUE

Writing down my interactions with the Sidhe was a strong invitation for me to look at where I stand in life — why I do what I do — and what I want to change. I decided to look at my contribution to raising others' vibration and that of myself. I revisited my activities, especially the source of my motivations to do what I am doing.

While I was in the editing phase of this book, Jeanne performed a Gaia session for me. In such a session, a person sets an intention. All that is needed to give form to that intention is available within Gaia. Jeanne's ability to connect to both the person and to Gaia allows for shifts and insights in a way I have never before experienced. The subject I wanted more clarity about was my work with crystal skulls and how it could help in the process of contributing to the development of a new consciousness. The experiences are particularly relevant to the content of this book; therefore, I am sharing them in this epilogue.

GAIA ON CRYSTAL SKULLS

In the beginning of the session, I only saw a big crystal skull. It was staring at me as if it were trying to convey a message to me. I could not hear the message. After a while, the image disappeared and only then did I receive a message.

A crystal skull is a physical symbol that represents two forms of consciousness: human consciousness and crystalline consciousness.

Because you are so locked in the physical form, you work with limited aspects of both types of consciousness. The symbol of the crystal skull helps you to remember that there is more than the consciousness of which you are aware. The crystal skull is a symbol that invites you to expand.

Many people on their spiritual paths believe that the focus needs to be on spirituality and not so much on physicality. When you make the decision to raise your vibration, this belief is a big mistake. You do not raise your vibration through spiritual aspects alone but through bringing the spiritual aspects into the physical being. To do this, the physical system needs to be cleared from all vibrations that have been induced by beliefs and emotions and that are not in alignment with your true essence. Once you begin to clear these vibrations from your physical system, more of your soul vibration can come through, which will raise the vibration of your total system.

The vibrations that can most powerfully support this process are the crystalline energies. The crystalline energies are the foundation of all life within the Gaia system. Reconnecting with crystalline consciousness helps you in your process and also helps Gaia as a whole.

Crystal skulls are not solely a symbol for the new consciousness. They also have the ability to help you to reconnect to the fields that are needed for this process. Crystal skulls are one of the most optimal support systems that can help you to connect with both the morphogenetic grids and the morphogenetic field. It is your consciousness that decides with which one you will connect. In this moment, your consciousness still holds you in the grid. However, working with crystal skulls to raise your vibration will bring you to the point in which they can help you to change your connection from the morphogenetic grid to the morphogenetic field. That is the gift of the crystal skulls.

In your world, many people give value to the age of crystal skulls. Ancient crystal skulls are often seen as more important than the ones that have been recently created. However, the key is to learn to work with both crystalline consciousness and human consciousness. The age of the crystal skulls is irrelevant to that process. Yes, you can learn from what has happened in the past. However, your vibrational state and the level of functional consciousness determine which energies and information you can access. If you can access this with an ancient crystal skull, you will also be able to access it with a contemporary skull. Realize that the skull is a symbol that helps you to connect and raise your vibration. There is no fundamental difference in potential between ancient and contemporary crystal skulls.

While it might seem that this information is old, it felt different to me. I felt that the information had a new depth that gave me the insight that the level at which I was working with crystal skulls was too limited. I felt new inspiration to continue with crystal skulls and to go beyond that place that had previously represented the maximum energy level. I felt new avenues of exploration and expansion had opened.

I knew at that moment, without a shadow of a doubt, that all the work I had done with crystal skulls was a valuable foundation for my contribution to the development of a new consciousness. Now I could feel what I had read once: Crystal skulls hold all that is needed to create a new human being. Let everyone who feels a connection with crystal skulls be inspired and explore new ways to use crystal skulls as tools for the birth of a new consciousness.

The information in this epilogue is in no way meant to give the crystal skulls more importance than the other possible connections and avenues that are mentioned in image 13.1. It is disclosed because it reflects that the energies of sharing with the Sidhe induce possibilities for shifts that you can experience in whatever way is most relevant to you. Let the energies of the connection with the Sidhe stimulate you to go to places you did not dare go before.

NOTES

Introduction

1. John Matthews, *The Sidhe, Wisdom from the Celtic Otherworld* (Everett, Washington: Lorian Press, 2004).
2. David Spangler, *Conversations with the Sidhe* (Camano Island, Washington: Lorian Press, 2014).
3. Richard Cassaro, "America's Orwellian Nightmare: Seven Ways to Awaken and Remember Who You Are," http://www.RichardCassaro.com/americas-orwellian-nightmare-seven-ways-to-awaken-and-remember-who-you-are accessed, December 5, 2014.
4. Jaap van Etten, *Crystal Skulls: Expand Your Consciousness* (Flagstaff, Arizona: Light Technology Publishing, 2013), 166–167.
5. For example, see the following video on the Heart Math Institute website: www.HeartMath.org/about-us/about-us-home/hearts-intuitive-intelligence.html, accessed December 8, 2014.

Chapter 1

1. *Lebor Gabála Érenn*, known in English as *The Book of Invasions* or *The Book of Conquests*, is a collection of poems and prose narratives that purports to be a history of Ireland from the creation of the world to the Middle Ages. See http://En.Wikipedia.org/wiki/Lebor_Gabála_Érenn, accessed December 8, 2014.
2. The *Tuatha Dé Danann* is a race of supernaturally gifted people in Irish mythology. They are thought to represent the main deities of pre-Christian Gaelic Ireland. See En.Wikipedia.org/wiki/Tuatha_Dé_Danann, accessed December 8, 2014.
3. *Aos sí* is the Irish term for a supernatural race in Irish and Scottish mythology. The members of this race are said to live underground in fairy mounds across the Western sea or in an invisible world that coexists with the world of humans. See En.Wikipedia.org/wiki/Aos_S%C3%AD, accessed December 8, 2014.
4. *Elfquest* is a cult hit comic book property created by Wendy and Richard Pini in 1978. It is a fantasy story about a community of elves and other fictional species who struggle to survive and coexist on a primitive Earth-like planet with two moons. See En.Wikipedia.org/wiki/Elfquest, accessed December 8, 2014.

5. David Spangler has written two books about the Sidhe: David Spangler and Jeremy Berg, *A Midsummer's Journey with the Sidhe* (Everett, Washington: Lorian Press, 2011). David Spangler, *Conversations with the Sidhe* (Camano Island, Washington: Lorian Press, 2014).
6. Jaap van Etten, *Gifts of Mother Earth: Earth Energies, Vortexes, Lines and Grids* (Flagstaff, Arizona: Light Technology Publishing, 2011), 144–148.
7. Ibid., 175–190.
8. David Spangler and Jeremy Berg, *Card Deck of the Sidhe* (Everett, Washington: Lorian Press, 2011).
9. Speaking of the glyph shown to John Matthews and discussed in his book, *The Sidhe, Wisdom from the Celtic Otherworld* (Everett, Washington: Lorian Press, 2004).

Chapter 2

1. Jaap van Etten, *Gifts of Mother Earth: Earth Energies, Vortexes, Lines, and Grids* (Flagstaff, Arizona: Light Technology Publishing, 2011).
2. Ibid, 175–190
3. There have been many preparations to start the Oneness project. However, there are many aspects to it, and I haven't had the time to start the project fully. *Birth of a New Consciousness* is undoubtedly part of it. Guidance will help with the future steps.

Chapter 3

1. Jaap van Etten, *Crystal Skulls: Expand Your Consciousness* (Flagstaff, Arizona: Light Technology Publishing, 2013), 137-162.
2. Jaap van Etten, *Gifts of Mother Earth: Earth Energies, Vortexes, Lines, and Grids* (Flagstaff, Arizona: Light Technology Publishing, 2011), 191-200.
3. Jaap van Etten, *Crystal Skulls: Expand Your Consciousness* (Flagstaff, Arizona: Light Technology Publishing, 2013), 142-151.
4. David Spangler, *Conversations with the Sidhe* (Camano Island, Washington: Lorian Press, 2014), 157-163.

Chapter 5

1. Kaplan, Aryeh, *Sefer Yetzirah: The Book of Creation* (Boston, Massachusetts: Weiser Books, 1997).

Chapter 6

1. Jaap van Etten, *Gifts of Mother Earth: Earth Energies, Vortexes, Lines, and Grids* (Flagstaff, Arizona: Light Technology Publishing, 2011), 45–53.
2. Ibid., 61–81.
3. Jaap van Etten, "The Gift of the Sedona Lemurian Landscape Temple," *Sedona Journal of Emergence!* vol. 24, no. 10 (2014), 65–71.
4. Jaap van Etten, *Gifts of Mother Earth: Earth Energies, Vortexes, Lines, and Grids* (Flagstaff, Arizona: Light Technology Publishing, 2011), 74-80.
5. Ibid., 47–53.

Chapter 7

1. Georgia Purdom and Dr. David Menton, "Did People Like Adam and Noah Really Live Over 900 Years of Age?" Answers in Genesis website, May 27, 2010, https://answersingenesis.org/bible-timeline/genealogy/did-adam-and-noah-really-live-over-900-years/, accessed on February 8, 2015.
2. Amy Norton, "Research: 'Longevity Gene' One Key to Long Life," Web MD, 2014, www.WebMD.com/cholesteral-management/news/20141106/longevity-gene-one-key-to-long-life-research-suggests, accessed December 11, 2014.

Chapter 9

1. Jaap van Etten, *Crystal Skulls: Expand Your Consciousness* (Flagstaff, Arizona: Light Technology Publishing, 2013), 164-165.

Chapter 10

1. This refers to the following two books: Jaap van Etten, *Crystal Skulls: Interacting with a Phenomenon* (Flagstaff, Arizona: Light Technology Publishing, 2007). Jaap van Etten, *Crystal Skulls: Expand Your Consciousness* (Flagstaff, Arizona: Light Technology Publishing, 2013).
2. Jaap van Etten, *Crystal Skulls: Expand Your Consciousness* (Flagstaff, Arizona: Light Technology Publishing, 2013), 119-120.
3. Ibid., 172-174

Chapter 11

1. David Bohm has written many interesting books on the implicate order: David Bohm, *Wholeness and the Implicate Order* (Routledge: London and New York), 1980. David Bohm & B. J. Hiley, *The Undivided Universe* (Routledge: London and New York), 1993.
2. There are several books on this subject, for example: Deborah Lipp, *The Way of Four: Create Elemental Balance in Your Life* (St. Paul, Minnesota: Llewellyn Publications, 2004). Cait Johnson, *Earth, Water, Fire & Air: Essential Ways of Connecting with Spirit* (Woodstock, Vermont: Skylight Paths Publishing, 2003).
3. For more information, visit our website, www.Lemurantis.com.

Chapter 13

1. M. Night Shyamalan, *After Earth* (Culver City, California: Sony Pictures, 2013). Movie starring Will and Jaden Smith.
2. Jaap van Etten, *Mother Earth and Dragons: A path to Mastering Physical Reality* (forthcoming).
3. The two books are: Jaap van Etten, *Crystal Skulls: Interacting with a Phenomenon* (Flagstaff, Arizona: Light Technology Publishing, 2007). Jaap van Etten, *Crystal Skulls: Expand Your Consciousness* (Flagstaff, Arizona: Light Technology Publishing, 2013).
4. David Spangler, *Subtle Worlds: An Explorer's Field Notes* (Everett, Washington: Lorian Press, 2010).
5. For more information, visit our website, www.Lemurantis.com.
6. John Matthews, *The Sidhe: Wisdom from the Celtic Otherworld* (Everett, Washington: Lorian Press, 2004).
7. David Spangler and Jeremy Berg, *Card Deck of the Sidhe* (Everett, Washington: Lorian Press, 2011).

ABOUT THE AUTHOR

Jaap van Etten, PhD, was born and educated in the Netherlands. He received his PhD in biology in Amsterdam, specializing in ecology. For the past twenty years, his focus has been on metaphysical ecology. He studies and teaches about human, Earth, stone, crystal, and crystal skull energies, and how these energies interact. He is the author of *Crystal Skulls: Interacting with a Phenomenon, Crystal Skulls: Expand Your Consciousness,* and *Gifts of Mother Earth.* Since  1998, he has lived in the United States with his wife, Jeanne Michaels. They currently reside in Sedona, Arizona.

𝄞 *Light Technology* PUBLISHING *Presents*

NICHOLAS R. MANN

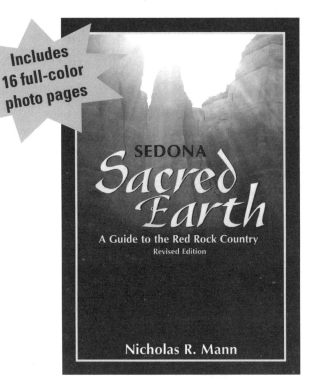

Includes 16 full-color photo pages

Sedona: Sacred Earth
A Guide to the Red Rock Country

This completely revised and updated edition looks at the spectacular landmarks of Arizona's Red Rock Country and suggests some startling new interpretations. Investigation into Native American legends and the application of ideas drawn from geomancy, philosophy, and vortex physics lead to the emergence of patterns of alignments, and sacred sites, as well as vast geometrical and animal figures in the Sedona landscape.

$14.95 • Softcover • 176 PP. • 6 x 9 Perfect Bound • ISBN 978-1-891824-45-6

THE ANCIENT SECRET
OF THE FLOWER OF LIFE,
VOLUME 1

Once, all life in the universe knew the Flower of Life as the creation pattern, the geometrical design leading us into and out of physical existence. Then from a very high state of consciousness, we fell into darkness, the secret hidden for thousands of years, encoded in the cells of all life.

Now, we are rising from the darkness, and a new dawn is streaming through the windows of perception. This book is one of those windows. Drunvalo Melchizedek presents in text and graphics the Flower of Life workshop, illuminating the mysteries of how we came to be.

Sacred geometry is the form beneath our being and points to a divine order in our reality. We can follow that order from the invisible atom to the infinite stars, finding ourselves at each step. The information here is one path, but between the lines and drawings lie the feminine gems of intuitive understanding.

You may see them sparkle around some of these provocative ideas:
- Remembering our ancient past
- The secret of the Flower unfolds
- The darker side of our present/past
- The geometries of the human body
- The significance of shape and structure

$25⁰⁰ Softcover, 240 PP.
ISBN 978-1-891824-17-3

Drunvalo Melchizedek's life experience reads like an encyclopedia of breakthroughs in human endeavor. He studied physics and art at the University of California at Berkeley, but he feels that his most important education came after college. In the past twenty-five years, he has studied with over seventy teachers from all belief systems and religious understandings. For some time now, he has been bringing his vision to the world through the Flower of Life program and the Mer-Ka-Ba meditation. This teaching encompasses every area of human understanding, explores the development of humankind from ancient civilizations to the present time, and offers clarity regarding the world's state of consciousness and what is needed for a smooth and easy transition into the twenty-first century.

THE ANCIENT SECRET
OF THE FLOWER OF LIFE,
VOLUME 2

The sacred Flower of Life pattern, the primary geometric generator of all physical form, is explored in even more depth in this volume, the second half of the famed Flower of Life workshop. The proportions of the human body; the nuances of human consciousness; the sizes and distances of the stars, planets, and moons; and even the creations of humankind are all shown to reflect their origins in this beautiful and divine image. Through an intricate and detailed geometrical mapping, Drunvalo Melchizedek shows how the seemingly simple design of the Flower of Life contains the genesis of our entire third-dimensional existence.

From the pyramids and mysteries of Egypt to the new race of Indigo children, Drunvalo presents the sacred geometries of the reality and the subtle energies that shape our world. We are led through a divinely inspired labyrinth of science and stories, logic and coincidence, on a path of remembering where we come from and the wonder and magic of who we are.

Finally, for the first time in print, Drunvalo shares the instructions for the Mer-Ka-Ba meditation, step-by-step techniques for the re-creation of the energy field of the evolved human, which is the key to ascension and the next dimensional world. If done from love, this ancient process of breathing prana opens up for us a world of tantalizing possibility in this dimension, from protective powers to the healing of oneself, of others, and even of the planet.

Topics Include:
- The Unfolding of the Third Informational System
- Whispers from Our Ancient Heritage
- Unveiling the Mer-Ka-Ba Meditation
- Using Your Mer-Ka-Ba
- Connecting to the Levels of Self
- Two Cosmic Experiments
- What We May Expect in the Forthcoming Dimensional Shift

$25⁰⁰ Softcover, 272 PP.
ISBN 978-1-891824-21-0